NEEDLE FELTED
Tapestries

MAKE YOUR OWN WOOLEN MASTERPIECES

Neysa Russo

STACKPOLE BOOKS

Guilford, Connecticut

Stackpole Books
An imprint of Globe Pequot

Distributed by
NATIONAL BOOK NETWORK
800-462-6420

British Library Cataloguing in Publication Information Available

Library of Congress Cataloging-in-Publication Data
Names: Russo, Neysa.
Title: Needle felted tapestries : design and make your own woolen
    masterpieces / By Neysa Russo.
Description: First edition. | Mechanicsburg, PA : Stackpole Books, 2017. |
    Includes bibliographical references and index.
Identifiers: LCCN 2015023201 | ISBN 9780811716086 (alk. paper)
Subjects: LCSH: Felt work. | Felting.
Classification: LCC TT849.5 .R87 2017 | DDC 746/.0463—dc23 LC record available at
http://lccn.loc.gov/2015023201

♾™ The paper used in this publication meets the minimum requirements of American National Standard for Information Sciences—Permanence of Paper for Printed Library Materials, ANSI/NISO Z39.48-1992.

Table of Contents

Introduction

Welcome to the world of needle felting! This book introduces you to the materials and methods of needle felting and presents a wide variety of projects, suitable for both the beginner and the experienced needle felter. The projects are designed to start simply and get progressively more challenging. Along the way, you will build your needling skills, gain design experience, and experiment with color. You will learn all the skills you need to design and create unique and personal felted items for your home.

Whether you have felted before or not, the fun projects in this book will inspire you and provide ideas for a lifetime of creative felt making. Be adventurous and have a great time!

PART I

All About Needle Felting

Materials & Tools

PRE-FELT

Pre-felt is the starting point for tapestry needle felting; it is used as the base for the projects in this book, and will be your "blank canvas." Pre-felt is wool that has been only partially felted and is therefore less dense. It may be manufactured or handmade.

Machine-made pre-felt is a lightly needled, loose fabric. It is usually a very fine, delicate sheet of wool and should be handled gently. It increases in density and durability when exposed to agitation through wet felting. Manufactured pre-felt is available in a wide range of colors, and since felt is a nonwoven fabric, it may be cut to any size or shape without unraveling. Be certain that the pre-felt you purchase is 100% wool. Because it is such a delicate fabric, I often recommend two layers for the projects in this book.

Handmade pre-felt is partially felted wool which has not been fully agitated and will also work beautifully as your blank canvas. The Maple Leaf Coaster project in this book teaches you how to make your own pre-felt from carded wool.

NEEDLES

Felting needles come in many gauges with variations related to the configuration, quantity, and depth of the barbs. The work of the needle is done on the bottom inch. As you poke the wool down with the needle, the barbs grasp strands of fiber, pushing them through the pre-felt base and securing them in the needling board underneath.

The best way to get familiar with the variety of needles that exists is by trying them. Besides the arrangement and depth of the barbs, other performance factors include the thickness of your pre-felt, the type of wool that you are using, and whether you are creating flat or three dimensional needle felt.

The 38 gauge needle with a triangular configuration is a great general purpose needle and is used to create most of the projects in this book. A needle with a star configuration is used for both of the three dimensional projects in the book. These needles have more barbs; therefore they push more fiber and work quickly and efficiently when shaping a form.

Felting tools

How to Use Felting Needles

To use a felting needle, pinch it between your thumb and finger and poke straight up and down through the pre-felt, landing well into the needling board. You may adjust the placement of fiber by poking at an angle, but you must pull the needle out of the needling board at the same angle it was inserted or it may break.

You will know you have the wrong needle for the job when:

- The needle struggles to penetrate the wool, requiring more effort on your part.
- The needle glides too easily through the wool, not catching enough strands. This causes you to do more of the repetitive poking motion with less result.

Felting needles are made of carbon steel and are brittle; therefore they will break if mishandled. Be certain to disinfect any wounds, and remember to secure your needles safely when you leave the work area.

Needling is a repetitive motion that could cause stress to your hand. There are several ways to minimize this.

- Be sure the needling board is only an inch thick.
- Support your arm and elbow by resting them on the table during needling.
- Let go of the needles each time you add more color.
- Stretch your fingers and move your hands often.
- Use the correct needle gauge for the job.

The more the wool is needled, the better the finished product will look. Needling strengthens the structure of the pre-felt by adding density. It also secures the fibers in place and prepares the design for wet felting. The more needling you have done to your design, the less likely it is that the fibers will float or shift during wet felting.

Check to see if you have needled enough by:

- Running your hand over the surface to check for shifting fibers; if you see any movement, needle that area more.
- Turning your design over. Felting needles push some of the fiber through, and your design should be clearly distinguishable on the back. If you see a weak area, turn it back over and needle that spot some more, adding more fiber where needed.
- Holding the pre-felt up to the light to reveal any weak areas.

NEEDLING BOARD

You must have a needling board under your project as you work so that the needle has a place to land safely as it penetrates the wool and pushes the fiber through the felt. Since the barbs are located on the bottom inch of the needle, the needling board should be 1 inch thick.

The needling board I used in these projects is "blue board" foam insulation used in housing construction. I often use that as my needling board because:

- It is inexpensive and readily available at the local lumberyard.
- It provides a firm, solid background—other needling boards may force your wrist and hand to bounce.

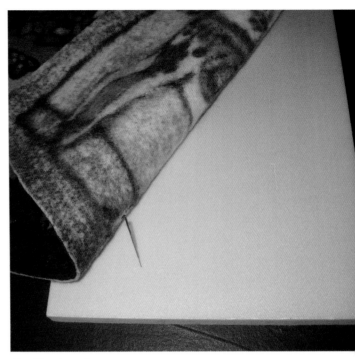

Needling board

- It is available in the ideal 1-inch thickness that I like. If your needling board is less than 1 inch thick, the needle may not be able to push the fiber far enough through and may break if it hits the work table underneath. Needling boards that are thicker than 1 inch may force your wrist upward, creating an awkward and uncomfortable needling position for your hand.
- It may be cut to any size.

Foam needling boards sold by felting retailers may be adequate for smaller projects, but as the size of the project increases, you will need a larger needling board, and insulation board is a good option.

Whichever you choose, you should be aware that the boards degrade with use and will occasionally need to be replaced. It is time to replace the board when you see that the barbs on the needle begin pulling small bits of the board up and they are sticking to the back of the felt. You will also feel a difference with each poke of the needle. Ideally, the needle penetrates the pre-felt, pushing the surface color with it. The surface fiber is secured into the board when the needle pushes it through; if your board is worn down, the fiber will not secure.

During the needling process some of the fiber lands in the board. It is important to gently lift and remove the project from time to time during your work, rotating it often to prevent it from adhering solidly to the board.

NEEDLING WOOL

Many types of needle felting wool are available and they come in a wide range of colors. Wool is processed in different ways, and beginners may be confused by the choices. To ensure success when completing the projects in this book, the wool you select should be from the same mill blend or from the same breed of sheep. Each breed of sheep produces wool that has a different scale structure, and they do not always felt well together.

The wool should also be carded, not combed. When wool is carded, the strands of fiber are bent, allowing them to entangle with one another more easily.

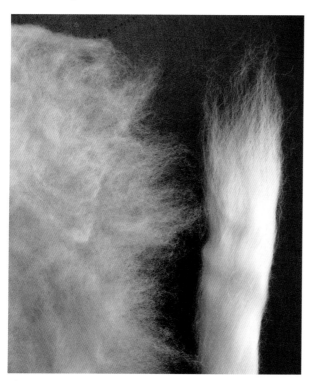

The wool fiber on the left is carded; the wool fiber on the right is combed.

The best wool for any project varies according to what you are trying to create, but for the projects in this book, carded wool with a short staple is ideal.

If you are new to felting, seeking advice from your retailer is a great way to learn about the fibers and what will work best for the type of felt you want to make.

Glossary of Fiber Preparation

Carded Fiber: The process of carding fiber mixes up the wool in a random fashion. The teeth on the carding machine bend the strands of fiber, making them receptive to entangling. This is the ideal wool to complete the projects in this book.

Combed Fiber (TOP): When wool is combed, it has been organized so that the fiber strands are parallel to one another. It is challenging to use in tapestry needle felting and requires special instruction for wet felting.

Batt: Fiber that is prepared in a batt has been carded into a sheet ready for felting. Layers may be lifted off or added on, so that you can felt thin or thick pieces or pull off small pieces for needling.

Roving: When wool is prepared in a strand it is called roving. Roving may be combed or carded.

Pencil Roving: A narrow strand of fiber prepared in the approximate diameter of a pencil. For the projects in this book, use carded pencil roving to create consistent lines.

How to Felt

WET FELTING

Wet felting is a simple process using hot water, soap, and pressure to force strands of wool to entangle and tighten, creating a dense fabric. Throughout the book you will be wet felting to finish the projects, lending durability to your needled designs. Each project may be wet felted using only your hand to create the agitation, but as the size of the projects increases, that can be time consuming. Using a tool with a textured surface is the key. The ridges and grooves of the various tools speed up the felting process.

WET FELT WORK STATION

Setting up a wet felting area on your kitchen countertop, in a bathroom, or in a laundry area will allow you easy access to hot tap water, drainage, and a surface that will not be harmed by excess water or soap. A counter or table also provides a comfortable height for your work station.

You will need a towel, plastic mat (a trash bag will work for the smaller projects, a pool cover or bubble wrap for the larger projects), and soap.

Lay down the towel to absorb any water run-off and to minimize the mess.

Put a piece of plastic on the towel. The plastic will hold in the water as the wool is wet down and should be slightly smaller than the towel in case you do have some excess water.

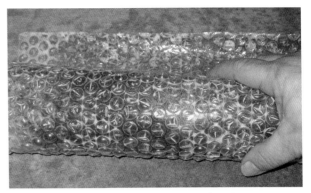

A felting roller is the ideal tool for the projects in this book. As the projects increase in size, and the need to maintain square edges is crucial, a felting roller becomes indispensable. You can purchase one or consider making one yourself with the instructions in this chapter.

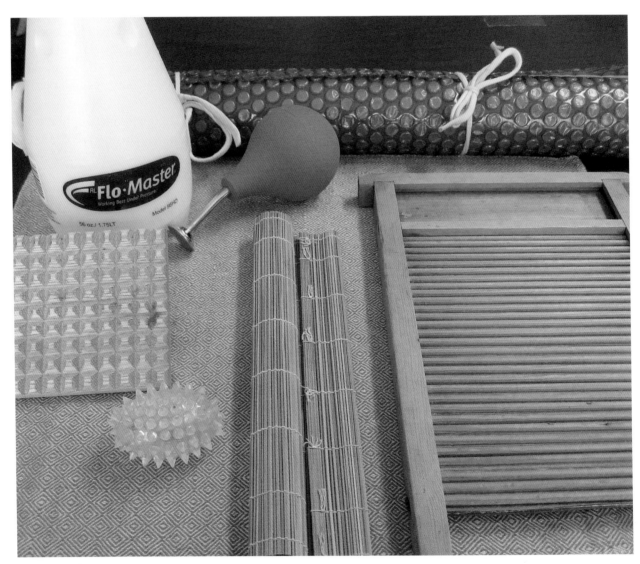

Wet felt work station

An old-fashioned washboard has a ridge pattern conducive to making fast work of wet felting. Use it in the sink so you have a place for the water to drain as you work.

A bamboo mat, often sold as a table placemat or window shade, provides texture and may be used instead of the pool cover or bubble wrap for rolling.

The FlashFelter is a handheld tool with ridges that cause agitation as you glide it over the flat surface of the felt.

A meat tenderizer also has a textured surface and is suitable for felting.

No matter what tools you are using to help you make felt, it is always best to begin the agitation with your hand to be sure the entire piece is well saturated.

Try out any of these tools to see what works best for you. Since some of them have aggressive surfaces, be sure that you:

- Use a nylon curtain to cover the surface of your felt until you are certain of how your tool will perform.
- Begin wet felting on the backside of the pre-felt, with the needled design face down.
- Saturate the pre-felt thoroughly with water.
- Add enough soap to allow your tool to glide freely over the surface.
- Begin with gentle agitation and gradually apply more pressure.
- Add more soap and hot water as needed.

WET FELT PROCESS

Once the wet felting work station is set up, you can begin to saturate your project with hot water.

Lay the needled design face down on the plastic—you will begin the wet felting on the backside. Fill a bowl with a few cups of hot tap water and keep it next to your felt.

Scrunch up a plastic grocery bag in your fist and dunk it in the bowl of water. Press the wet bag down onto the project, pushing the trapped water into the pre-felt. Repeat this process until the entire project is saturated.

For small projects, cradle the needled item in your hands and run it under the tap until it is saturated.

Use your hand to press down on the surface of the saturated fiber; if water pools around your fingers, you are ready to begin. Apply soap to your palm. This will act as a lubricant and allow your hand to glide smoothly over the surface. The continuous motion of your hand is agitating the fiber, causing the strands to entangle and the wool to shrink, eventually creating felt. If your

Felting with a Washboard

Pre-felt is a fragile material, and the weight of the water you added to saturate it could distort the shape until it has been exposed to some agitation from wet felting. You should always begin wet felting the projects in this book by using agitation created by gliding your hand over the surface for a few minutes.

Once you are able to handle the fabric without distorting the shape, place it on top of the washboard and gently slide it up and down the ridges, moving it around often to be sure it is felting evenly in all directions. Add more soap and hot water when needed to keep it moving smoothly. Gradually increase the amount of pressure you apply.

Because the ridges of a washboard provide excellent agitation, the felting process may happen quickly. Check for distortion frequently by laying the felt out flat. Many of the projects in this book require that the edges remain squared or the proportions of the original be retained, so if you have chosen to use a washboard it is important to continually keep an eye on the progress.

hand stops gliding smoothly, add more soap. Always begin the agitation gently, using either a circular or back and forth motion, and becoming increasingly aggressive. To be sure the project maintains its shape as it is shrinking, use an even amount of pressure in all areas. If one area shrinks more and distorts the shape, apply more agitation to the opposite area.

Too much water can hinder the wet felting process by causing the strands of fiber to swim past each other, not giving the scales the opportunity to entangle.

Shrinkage

You will see and feel the fibers of your project tighten and shrink as you agitate. The more aggressively and the longer you agitate, the tighter and smaller your felt will become. Each project gives an approximation of how long to wet felt and what to expect from shrinkage, but there are many variables and no firm formula. Some factors may include:

- What type of wool you use.
- How well you have needled. The more needling that is done, the denser the fabric will be.
- How aggressively you agitate.
- Whether you are using your hand, a washboard, or another textured surface to assist you.

Finishing

Stretching your finished wool to correct the proportions may work for small tweaks, but because wool has so much elasticity don't expect to correct huge errors in distortion. Your piece may always be wet down and felted some more. Repeating the wet felting process is also helpful if you find that you have not agitated sufficiently, you needled more wool in after the felting process, or if you simply need to clean it.

MAKE YOUR OWN FELT ROLLER

A felt roller is an essential tool for wet felting. It is made up of several parts:

Plastic pipe—The pipe provides a firm resistance during the wrap-and-roll process. It helps with the agitation by pushing out trapped air and forcing the strands of fiber to come in contact with one another. Your local lumber yard sells PVC waterpipe, which is very durable and may be cut to any length. I find the 1½-inch diameter pipes to be a perfect size for small and large projects.

A plastic textured mat—The mat should be slightly larger than the pre-felt you are going to wet out. A piece of a swimming pool cover is used with the projects in this book. As a beginner, you may use regular bubble wrap with small bubbles, but it may need to be replaced often. Check with your local swimming pool dealer to see if they have scraps, or check with the retailers listed in the back of the book.

Nylon curtain material—This should also be slightly larger than your felting project. The curtain is needed when wet felting raw fiber to make felt, as in the Maple Leaf Coaster project in this book. The curtain contains the fibers as you saturate the wool with hot water and will allow you to begin agitating without disturbing the wool. This material may be purchased as a hemmed curtain or by the yard.

Ties—Once the textured surface and felt are wrapped around the roller, use ties to hold them in place while you roll. These ties can be made from knee high stockings or spandex cloth which will stretch to suit the diameter of your rolled project.

WRAP AND ROLL INSTRUCTIONS

- Place a towel on your work surface to absorb excess water.
- Place the plastic mat, with the textured side down, on the towel.
- Place the needled design face down on the mat. If the project begins with raw wool, cover it with the nylon curtain.
- Saturate the project with hot water and gently agitate it with your soapy hands.
- Place the PVC pipe at one end of the project and roll the mat and the felt around the pipe. Excess water will be absorbed by the towel on the work station.
- Tie the roll, one tie on each end, and begin rolling it back and forth.

Rolling is done with your forearms. Rest your wrists on the roll and rotate the assembly toward your elbow and back to your wrists again using modest pressure. Do this for about ten minutes.

It is important that you move the placement of your wrists frequently so that the pressure you are applying is not in the same spot with every roll. Move your wrists a couple of inches each time you go back and forth with the roller. Imagine playing the length of a piano, moving your hands up and down the keyboard from side to side.

Unwrap the roll and rewrap it from the opposite end of the mat. Changing the direction of the agitation will help ensure that your project is felt-

ing evenly during the ten-minute rotation. Check to be sure that the pre-felt is still wet and soapy. If it is a large project, use a yardstick to be certain that the squared edges have maintained their proportions.

If one area is shrinking more than another, apply more pressure to the opposite area to bring it back to shape.

FELTING SOAP

Wet felting is hard on the hands. For that reason, olive oil soap is recommended, but most kinds of soap will work fine. Soaps contain an alkaline which may affect the pH balance of the wool, but for the purposes of these projects, it is not all that important. Further information is available on the subject from the titles listed in the bibliography.

When wet felting, the soap is used as a lubricant so that your hand (or any textured tool) can glide freely across the surface, ensuring the agitation needed to convert wool to felt. Whatever soap you use, be sure to rinse it thoroughly from the felt when finished.

Designing Your Piece

DESIGN TOOLS

Permanent markers are used as a sketching tool. If your marker is not permanent, it may wear off, bleed through, or smudge. Some of the projects in this book are drawn directly on the felt.

A ruler, a T-square, a yardstick, and a measuring tape are imperative for maintaining symmetry in your designs and, as you progress through the book, invaluable for creating borders on larger tapestries. They can also come in handy during wet felting to ensure that your felt is shrinking evenly.

Scissors are needed for cutting the felt. The sharper they are, the better, as the projects often require trimming the edges close to the needled designs.

INSPIRATION

Inspiration may be found everywhere. You might find ideas in nature, the people or pets around you, or by leafing through books. Part of the artistic process is the time spent in contemplation.

I have been inspired by antique textiles, samplers, embroidery and needlepoint patterns, graphed knitting charts, picture books, and coloring books—all provide endless ideas. I got inspiration for several projects in this book by looking at pictures of Middle Eastern rugs. The designs offer many ideas on background geometry, motifs, and beautiful color combinations. They provide inspiration and design ideas that may be modified to fit needle felting. With a little imagination, one idea or a single motif can become an entire tapestry.

Guardians at the Tree of Life. *This is an ancient theme that offers endless design possibilities.*

The Emperor on a Lion Hunt. *Inspired by an 8th century fabric remnant, this felt tapestry comes to life with vibrant colors and an action-packed scene.*

DESIGN

You do not need any formal training to create your own designs. As you gain needling skills and confidence through the progression of projects in this book, you will be inspired to design a project of your own. Be flexible as you turn your ideas into a felted masterpiece and see how a simple design idea transforms into a unique piece of art.

Never worry about doing something "wrong" in your design. Stay flexible, knowing that most of the errors we make as beginners are fixable. The more changes you make, and the more you are able to experiment, the more unique and wonderfully personal your artwork becomes.

Once you have your inspiration, there are a few simple ways to transfer your design to the pre-felt.

Tracing

Many beginners who do not feel artistic find it easier to trace a design on the pre-felt. Because manufactured pre-felt is such a lightweight and transparent fabric, transferring a design idea is simple. Make sure the drawing that you want to transfer has a nice bold outline and tape it to a window. Tape your pre-felt over it and use the natural light and a permanent marker to trace the picture on the pre-felt.

Quartering

If you are working from a photograph or an illustration, there is a simple technique that you can use. Create a grid on the picture. Make one line that intersects horizontally and one that intersects

vertically, meeting in the center. Apply the same grid to your pre-felt canvas. Be sure they are both proportionally the same. For example if your photograph is 4 x 6 inches, begin your canvas with a multiple of those numbers, like 16 x 24. That means your pre-felt will be four times larger than the photo. This simplifies the measuring process and minimizes the need for adjustments later on. Working from these smaller sections is more manageable. Remember to always cut your pre-felt larger to account for shrinkage during wet felting, plus a little extra edge for trimming and space to add a border that will frame your design.

Stencils

Make stencils with poster board and an X-Acto knife. Use a photocopier to reduce or enlarge the motif if desired. Glue the copy onto a piece of poster board and cut it out with the X-Acto knife.

Freestyle

Sketching your ideas on paper is a great way to get started, even if it's a simplistic "stick figure" design. This does not have to be an elaborate drawing but a basic idea of what will go where.

First, use a yardstick to create a squared border around the pre-felt. This will frame your tapestry and give you a clear visual of your design area.

If you are designing a landscape scene, needle down the colors of the background first. Your central or main idea may be centered on the pre-felt after that is done, needled right on top of the background to avoid any gaps in colors.

If you are working with a geometric design, draw the background geometry, as illustrated in several of the projects in this book, and needle the background colors. The details will be needled on top.

Taking Care of Felt

Wool felt is versatile, durable, and relatively easy to care for. Felt may be spot cleaned with hot water and soap. It may be touched up with more needling and even wet felted again at any time during its life. When damp, it can be tugged here and there to reshape, and since felt is not a woven fabric, it may be cut to any size or shape without unraveling.

PART II

The Projects

Flower Muq Rug

*T*he flower coaster is a simple project to get you started with tapestry needle felting. You will learn how to use the needles and experiment with your own creative color arrangements. It will also introduce you to the technique of wet felting to finish the project. Wet felting will tighten the fibers of the needled design, turning it to felt.

Materials

Wool

Pre-felt fabric in a light color
Carded wool fiber in any color combination

Felting Needle

38 triangular

*T*he medallion is a simple design element that is repeated in many of the more complex projects. It begins in the center with evenly spaced petals and is worked outward.

Use a small dinner plate or bowl approximately 10 inches wide as a template. Trace its outline on the pre-felt with a permanent marker and cut it out. Use two layers of pre-felt to create more density. Place the pre-felt discs together on top of the needling board so that the needle has a place to land when it punctures the wool. Start with a small amount of wool fiber, adding more as needed. If you use too large a chunk of wool, it will take more jabs and will take longer to needle down firmly. If you do not use enough wool, the design will be too transparent and you will need to add more wool to it.

Begin at the center of the pre-felt disk with a dab of yellow fiber. Pinch the top of the needle. Use a straight up and down poking motion, inserting the barbed end of the needle through the pre-felt and landing well into the needling board underneath. The bottom inch of the needle is barbed, and when you poke the wool, the barbs grasp strands of fiber and push some of the

carded wool through to the other side. The bottom inch of the needle must penetrate fully to maximize each poke.

Needle the wool into a circle about the size of a quarter.

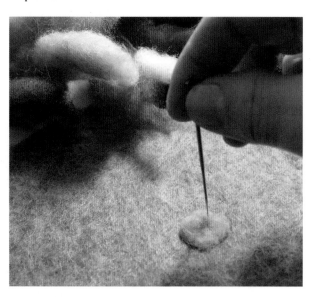

HELPFUL HINT:

Inserting the needle at an angle is a great way to adjust the placement of fiber, but be sure to pull it out at the same angle to prevent the needle from snapping.

Choose another color and create five evenly spaced petals around the center dot. Make them rounded at the top. Don't needle them down tightly until you are sure that all five will fit and are approximately the same size and shape.

Needle the next color, tightly bordering the first row of petals. There is no science to choosing colors, simply pick any combination you find pleasing.

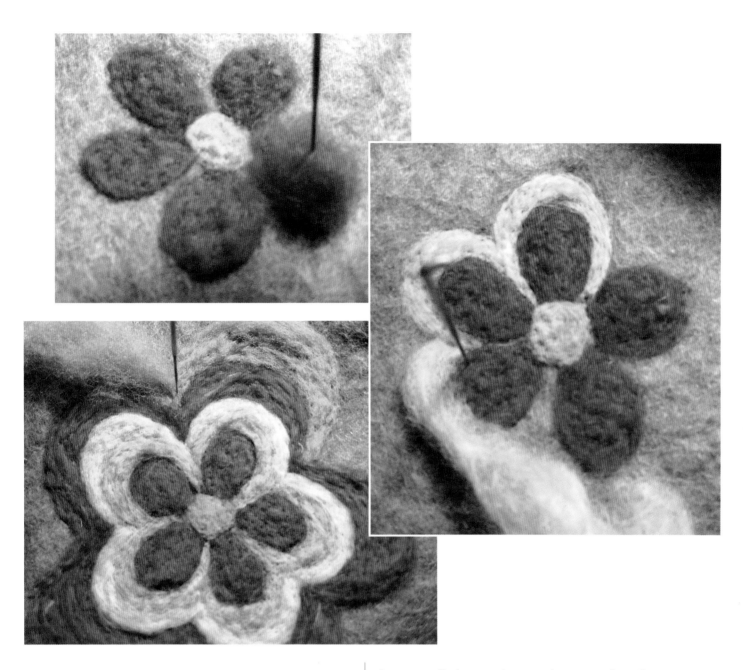

You will notice the pre-felt adhering to the needling board as you work. Lift it gently off and rotate it frequently during your progress. Pulling or tugging too hard at one corner may distort the shape.

Grow your flower outward with each new color addition. Each color change may be as wide or as narrow as you like until the flower has filled the felt disc.

Remember to needle the wool down gently at first, until you are certain of the colors and shapes you have created. If you change your mind about a design or a color and it has not been needled securely into place, simply pull it up gently. If it has been needled securely, needle the preferred color right over the old one.

Don't worry! There are always opportunities to change or correct things as you go through the needle felting process.

Once you have completed your design, check to see if the flower has been needled enough. Run your hand over the surface to check for shifting fibers; if you see any movement, needle that area more. Turn the flower over. Felting needles push some of the fiber through to the back. The design should be clearly distinguishable. If you see a weak area, turn it back over and needle that spot some more.

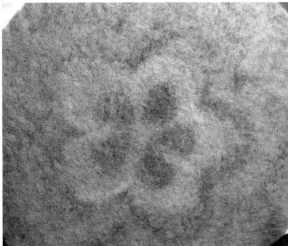

This is what the backside of your felt should look like.

Once you are satisfied that your design has been well needled, it is time to wet felt your project.

Set up a wet felting work station according to the instructions in the beginning of the book.

Cradle the needled flower in your hands as you saturate it with hot water from the tap. Place it face down on the plastic. Lay your hand flat on the flower and press gently. Water should pool around your fingers in all areas.

Put soap on the palm of your hand. The soap acts as a lubricant, allowing your hand to glide smoothly over the surface of the flower. Move your hand in a circular or back and forth motion, gently at first, then with increasing vigor. Be sure to cover all areas equally. The continuous motion of your hand is causing agitation, which is making felt. Add more soap or hot water as needed.

You will see and feel the fibers tighten and shrink, creating a dense fabric—felt. The amount it shrinks depends on many variables which are discussed in the beginning of the book. Agitate each side aggressively for about fifteen minutes. The more aggressively and longer you agitate, the tighter and smaller your felt will become.

Your flower should now measure approximately 9 inches across.

Rinse the flower under the tap to thoroughly remove the soap.

Use a hot iron to flatten and smooth both sides of the flower. Place a cloth between the iron and the felt to prevent burning and to absorb some of the moisture. Lay the flower flat to dry.

Strengthen any weak areas by needling in more fiber, or change a color if you need to by needling right on top of the old color—you can always wet felt it again!

During the wet felting process, strands of fiber from the base wool may migrate to the surface of the flower. If that occurs, once the flower is dry, shave the surface with a razor to clean it up. A lint roller works well to clean up any stray fibers. Trim the edges into shape with scissors. Because felt is not a woven material, it may be cut into any shape without unraveling.

The possibilities are endless for creating variety in your flowers, experimenting with different shapes and color combinations.

The nature of felt is forgiving and can be changed, repaired, or cleaned easily. If your felt flower needs to be cleaned, wash it by hand in warm soapy water.

The natural lanolin in wool creates a water resistant barrier perfect for your new coaster!

Needle and Pin Case

This is a fun project with lots of opportunity for playful design. Felting needles are capable of very precise detail which will help as you design small petals, vines, and leaves. This project makes a lovely gift that is sure to be appreciated for its beauty and practicality.

Materials

Wool

Black or dark-colored pre-felt
Dabs of any color carded fiber you have in your stash

Felting Needle

38 triangular

Finishing

Snap
Wool yarn
Tapestry needle
Sewing needle and thread

To begin the first vine, use a piece of green fiber to create an elongated "S" shape anywhere on the half that will be embellished. Later you will be stitching on a border around the outside edge, so leave a ¼-inch space between the design and the edge of the pre-felt.

Once you have completed the vine, add a colored dot at the end to make a flower center around which you can add the petals.

Create more flowers and vines, distributing the designs as evenly as possible without overlapping them.

Cut a circular piece of pre-felt approximately 6 inches in diameter. A bread plate or small bowl will work as stencils for tracing. Use two layers of pre-felt for this project.

Fold the circles in half and press in a crease with your fingers. The design in this project will only be on one half of the disk (of course you may cover the entire area if you like). The crease acts as a guide for how much design space you have. You might find that you need to press the crease again or even change the position of it slightly as you progress.

Unfold and lay the pre-felt disks together on top of the needling board.

DESIGN TIP:

Place a very small dab of a lighter color in the center of each petal to create a more elaborate design.

Make another elongated "S" shape and add more flowers. Once a flower is needled, fill in any empty space around it with a leaf, a partial flower, or a smaller vine.

You have used some really simple shapes to create an intricate looking design!

The outside border and half of the pre-felt disk do not have any needling (the negative space) and therefore have nothing to bind the two layers together. It is important to needle the two layers of pre-felt together before you begin to wet felt, otherwise they may not felt together. Needle lightly, all over the background and the border with a few taps of the needle—just enough to secure the two disks together.

Once your design is complete and the pre-felt layers are secured, it is time to wet felt the project.

Set up a wet felting work station according to the instructions in the beginning of the book. Saturate the disk with hot water from the tap and lay it face down on the plastic. Place your hand flat on the disk and press the surface gently. Water should pool around your fingers in all areas.

Put soap on the palm of your hand. The soap, acting as a lubricant, allows your hand to glide smoothly over the surface; rub gently at first, then with increasing vigor. The continuous

The design grows, shape by shape and color by color.

motion of your hand is agitating the fibers and causing the strands of wool to become entangled. Add more soap or water as needed. You will see and feel the fibers tighten and shrink, creating a dense felt fabric. The amount it shrinks depends on how much you continue to rub. Do each side aggressively for about ten to fifteen minutes or until the disk measures about 5½ inches in diameter. This is simply a guideline; don't worry if it is a bit smaller or larger.

Thoroughly rinse the disk under the tap to remove the soap, and use a hot iron on both sides to flatten and smooth the fibers. Place a cloth between the iron and the felt to prevent burning and to absorb some of the moisture. Trim the circumference of the circular disk with scissors to clean up the edges.

Fold the disk in half and, with the hot iron, press in the crease. Let it dry in that half-moon shape.

Cut a piece of wool yarn 2 yards long and thread it into a tapestry needle. Use the blanket stitch to create the embroidered edging all the way around the disk, spacing the stitches about ¼ inch apart.

To finish the project, sew one half of a snap at the center top on each side. Your needles and pins will be safe and secure in their new felt case.

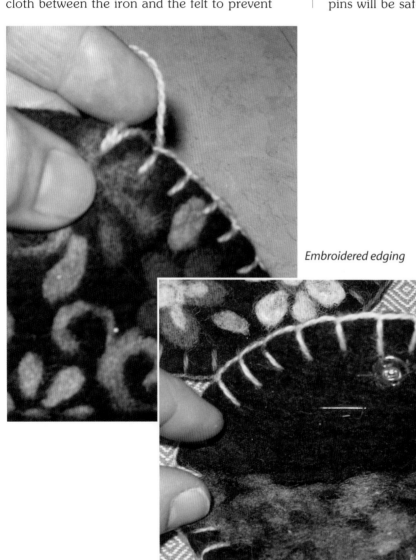

Embroidered edging

Sugar Skull

*S*ugar skulls are a quirky and simple project. They are great practice for creating balanced design in a limited space and will also demonstrate how the simplest shapes may combine to create elaborate looking designs!

Materials

Wool

Black or dark pre-felt
Any colors of carded fiber

Felting Needle

38 triangular

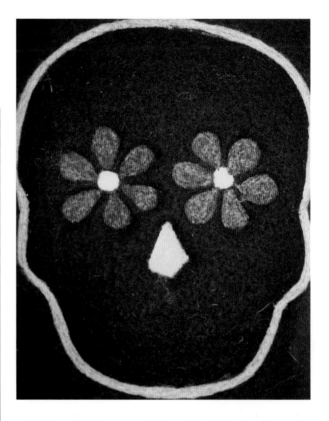

Trace the stencil, located in the back of the book, on the pre-felt. Use two layers of pre-felt for added durability.

Be sure you use a permanent marker. There is negative space (the background) that will not have any design, and using a permanent marker will prevent smudging or possible bleeding through of the ink. If your pre-felt is a dark color, use a metallic-colored permanent marker.

Choose an outline color of carded wool and pull off a section about the diameter of a pencil. Needle this wool over the permanent marker lines all the way around, adding more sections of wool as needed.

Remember, the bottom inch of the needle is where all the action is happening. The barbs on the needle grasp and push some of the strands of fiber through to the other side, so the needle must penetrate the pre-felt and land well into the needling board underneath. Use a straight up and down poking motion. To prevent the needle from snapping, be sure to pull it from the needling board at the same angle it was inserted.

Start with the eyes. They should be in the middle of the skull, spaced approximately 2 inches apart. To mark those locations use a ruler, then needle a circle of wool the size of a dime for each pupil. Create flower petals around the eye centers. Whether the petals are small or large, keep them evenly spaced around the centers.

Noses can be created in many sizes and shapes—a teardrop, an elongated diamond, or even a triangle like a jack-o-lantern. Nostrils can be simple circles on the sides of the nose.

As you needle, you will notice the pre-felt adhering to the needling board. Rotate it frequently by gently lifting it up from the board. Pulling or tugging too hard at one corner may distort your pre-felt shape. If it does become distorted, gently tug it back into shape before you continue.

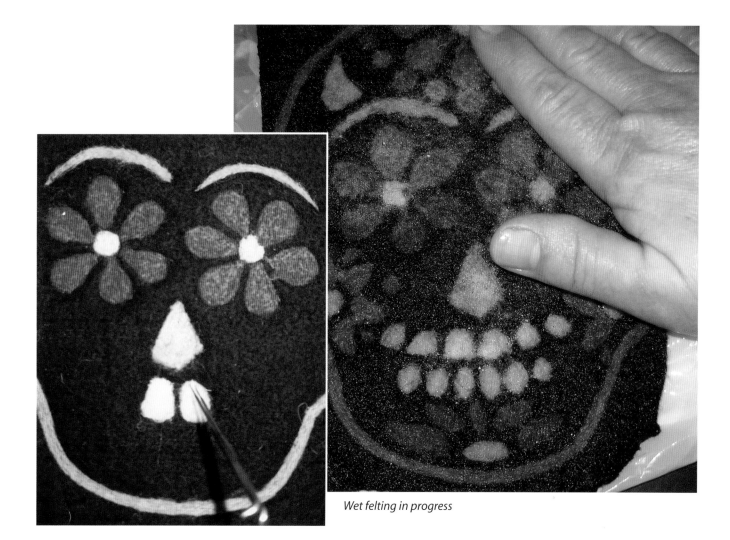

Wet felting in progress

For teeth, start with the top row and place the two front teeth below the nose and to the right and left. Create more teeth to complete the mouth, adding as few or as many as you like.

Continue needling your skull, distributing the design and maintaining the proportions evenly while filling the empty space with various shapes and colors for the chin, ears, and crown.

Follow along with this design or create your own. The skulls shown here are intended to get you started, but they leave lots of room for your own style and imagination. This project is a great way to experiment with color and design composition. The shapes are simple, but combine in various ways to look elaborate. Some common shapes found in sugar skulls are circles, flowers, hearts, crosses, and stars. As you gain confidence with needle felting, endless possibilities will unfold!

Set up a wet felting work station according to the instructions in the beginning of the book.

Cradle the skull in your hands as you saturate it with hot water from the tap, then place it on the plastic. Lay your hand flat on the skull and press gently. Water should pool around your fingers in all areas.

Put soap on your palm to allow your hand to glide over the surface easily. Begin rubbing the skull gently in a circular or back and forth motion and gradually increase the vigor of the movement. The continuous motion of your hand is agitating and locking the fibers together. You will see and feel the fibers tighten and shrink together, creating a dense felt fabric. Add more soap to your hand as needed. Work on each side aggressively for about ten to fifteen minutes.

When the wet felting is completed your skull will have shrunk about ½ inch. Don't worry if it is a bit smaller or larger. There are many variables to account for in wet felting and every person may have different shrinkage rates depending on how aggressively they wet felt, what type of wool was used, and how long the project was agitated. If you are not satisfied with the density of the felt fabric, it can always be felted some more.

Rinse the felted skull under the faucet to remove the soap. If the skull has become distorted during the wet felting process, try reshaping it by tugging gently while it is wet.

HELPFUL HINT:

Because of the elasticity of wool fiber, it is difficult to correct for large distortions unless you saturate it again and wet felt it some more. If your project has lost its symmetry, it means that you were more aggressive in one area. To correct this you should work the opposite area to bring it back into shape.

Use a hot iron on both sides to flatten and smooth the fibers. Place a cloth between the iron and the felt to prevent burning and to absorb some of the moisture. Lay the skull flat to dry.

If your design was not needled securely and fibers have shifted, you can always touch it up with more needling. Shave it with a razor to clean up any fibers that have migrated. Use a lint roller to clean up the surface if needed.

Trim the edges into shape with scissors. Because felt is not a woven material, it may be cut into any shape without unraveling.

If your felt skull needs a cleaning, simply wash by hand in warm soapy water.

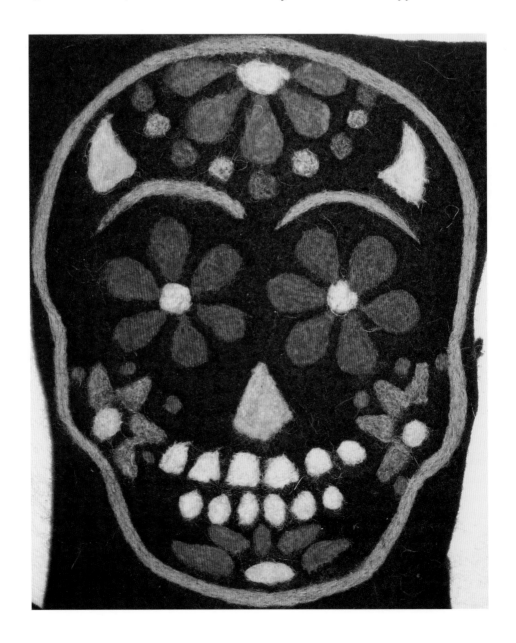

Wallet

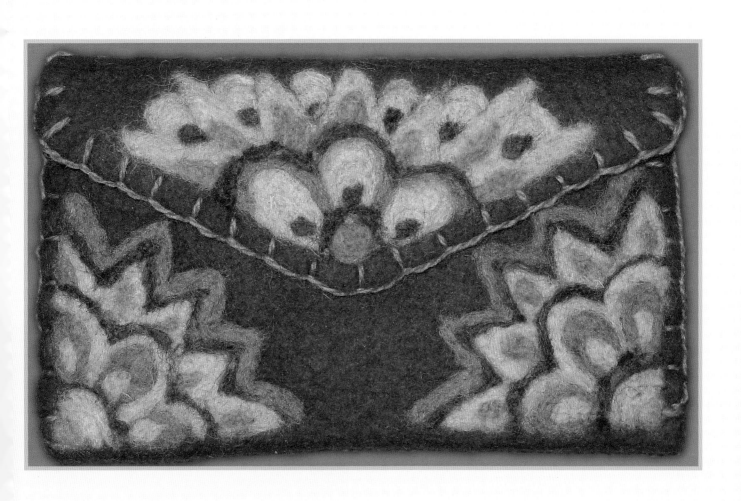

T̲his beautiful wallet has lots of room for flexibility in design, shape, and size. You will learn how to create a symmetrical design, using a ruler to keep yourself centered. You will also learn how to maintain those square edges during the wet felting process.

Materials

Wool

Pre-felt in any color
Carded wool in any color. This sample used Harrisville Designs fiber in Seagreen, Lime, Goldenrod, Hemlock, Spruce, Sand, and Grass.

Felting Needle

38 triangular

Finishing

Wool yarn
Tapestry needle
Lining fabric, if desired
Snap
Sewing needle and thread

U̲se two layers of pre-felt for this project to make your wallet more durable.

Use a ruler and a permanent marker to be sure you have nice straight lines, and cut out a rectangle measuring 6 x 9 inches (for the example wallet here) or any size that you prefer.

DESIGN TIP:

Make this item in any size! Create a sleeve for your cell phone, tablet, or e-reader, or add a zipper or a clasp for a purse. You won't be able to make just one!

Cut the top inch of the rectangle into a "V" shape, similar to an envelope.

Fold the pre-felt into three sections and press the creases with an iron. It will be helpful in the needling process to know how much design space you have within each section.

Unfold and place the two layers of pre-felt on the needling board.

The bottom inch of the needle is where all the work is happening. The barbs on the needle grasp the carded wool and push some of the strands through to the backside, so the needle must penetrate the pre-felt and go well into the needling board underneath.

HELPFUL HINT:

Remember to use a straight up and down poking motion with the needle. Inserting the needle at an angle is a great way to adjust the placement of fiber, but be sure to pull it out at the same angle to prevent the needle from snapping.

Begin with the triangular flap and needle a center dot. Create three evenly spaced petals, which, by now, you are an expert at making.

Work outward with more petals and more colors in your own design, or re-create this rising sun design with bursts of triangles. The simplest

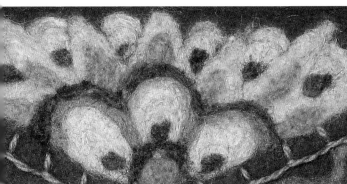

Measuring for symmetry

shapes can create elaborate looking designs. Consider each section of the fold an opportunity for a different design.

You will notice the pre-felt adhering to the needling board. Rotate it frequently by gently lifting it off the board. Pulling too hard at one corner may distort the pre-felt shape. If it does become distorted, gently tug it back into shape before continuing.

It is helpful to know where the flap will rest when the wallet is closed, as it gives a clearer picture of the design area. Mark this line by needling it a few times. Use a ruler to create symmetrical shapes and maintain an evenly composed design.

When all the needling is tight and complete, it is time to wet felt your wallet.

Set up a wet felting area according to the instructions located in the beginning of the book.

Lay the wallet on the plastic with the design side down. Fill a bowl with a few cups of hot water and keep it next to your felt. Scrunch up a plastic grocery bag in your fist and submerge it in the hot water, then place the bag over the wallet. Press down, releasing the trapped water onto the wallet. The lanolin in wool is naturally resistant to water, so pressing it in helps the saturation process.

The wallet is ready for some agitation when you press down on it and water pools around your fingers in all areas. Put soap on the palm of your hand to act as a lubricant, allowing your hand to glide over the surface easily. The continuous motion of your hand is agitating the wool and forcing the strands of fiber to entangle. Add more water or soap as needed to keep your hand gliding smoothly. You will see and feel the fibers tighten and shrink, creating a dense felt fabric. The amount it shrinks depends on how forcefully you agitate it and for how long. Work on each side aggressively for at least fifteen minutes or until it measures approximately 5½ x 8½ inches. Rinse the wallet under the faucet, removing the soap thoroughly.

Your pre-felt will shrink during the wet felt process as the fibers tighten together. To be sure it retains its shape, keep the wallet flat and use an even amount of pressure in all areas, checking periodically with a ruler. If one area shrinks more and distorts the wallet shape, try applying extra agitation to the opposite areas to bring it back in line.

If the felt has become distorted after the wet felting is complete, try reshaping it by tugging gently while it is wet. You could also wet it out again and felt it some more. If your design was not needled securely and fibers have shifted, you can touch it up with more needling or shave it with a razor. Trim the edges with scissors to clean them up, and then use a lint roller over the surface to clean up any stray fibers.

Fold the felt back into the envelope shape, press the creases with a hot iron, and let it dry.

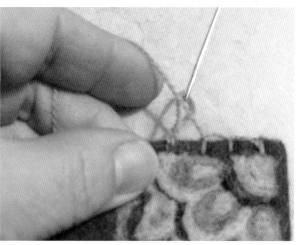

Hand stitching the sides adds a nice design element. Cut a piece of wool yarn 2 yards long and thread it into a tapestry needle. Use the blanket stitch to create an embroidered edging all the way around the wallet, spacing stitches about ¼ inch apart.

For a more professional look, line the wallet with fabric before using a sewing machine to close it up.

Sew on a snap to complete.

If your wallet needs to be cleaned, wash it by hand in warm soapy water.

Hand stitched edges and a snap are the final touches.

Choir Angel Ornament

These beautiful ladies are so much fun to create you will find it hard to make just one!

Materials

Wool

Any color pre-felt
Carded fiber in colors of your choice

Felting Needle

38 triangular

Finishing

1-inch varnished wooden ball with a hole through the center
2 Pipe cleaners
Glue gun
Locks of wool for hair
Fine permanent markers
Bells for the hands
Ribbon for hanging

Dress

Use the template located in the back of the book.

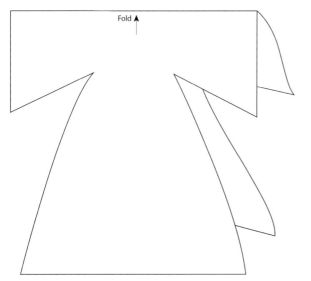

Fold your pre-felt in half. Place the top of the stencil on that fold and trace it with a permanent marker. Cut it out but don't cut the fold!

Lay the dress out flat on the needling board. The design will only be on the front half of the dress.

Begin anywhere—the possibilities are endless for exciting dress designs! See some examples at the end of this chapter, or create your own based on the skills you have already learned.

DESIGN TIP:

If you are stumped for ideas, consider different styles of dresses, eras, or ethnic backgrounds—high empire waists, southern ball gowns, Japanese kimonos, Russian peasants, or Native Americans. Don't forget the accessories! Aprons, scalloped borders, stripes or floral designs, layered skirts, sashes, belts, necklaces, and robes can all add pizzazz to your design.

This project does not require the extra durability of wet felting. After needling the design on the dress, check to see if it has been needled enough by gliding your hand over the surface to

Preparing the dress

Use your imagination when it comes to the dolls' faces

check for shifting fibers; if you see any movement, needle that area more. When the design is complete, use a hot iron and a damp cloth to press the back. Fold the dress in half and press the front, smoothing the needled fibers flat. The hot iron will also remove a lot of the needle marks. Trim any fuzzy edges and put the dress aside until the head is complete.

Face

If the wooden ball you are using has not been varnished, you may want to consider doing it. Varnish prevents the ink from running or spreading, allowing for a crisp and clean fine line.

Use a fine point, permanent black marker to draw a face on the wooden ball.

First, draw two almond-shaped eyes in the center of the head, making them one eye length apart. Place a dot in the center of each eye for the pupil. With a blue or green fine-tip marker, draw a tiny circle around the black dot in the center of the almond. Create some brows with an arc above the eyes.

The nose between the eyes looks like a backward check mark or an upside down number seven.

The mouth should extend from one eye center to the other. Outline the shape in black first, then fill in with red or pink. If your ornament will be a choir singer, make the mouth an oval shape and fill in with pink or red.

If you don't like what you have drawn, or you have made a mistake, turn the head and try again on the other side. Her hair will cover the mistake at the next stage. Practice on paper if that's helpful.

Thread the pipe cleaner through the head until the head rests in the center of the pipe cleaner. Bend the top half of the pipe cleaner over so that it is parallel with the other half. Hold the head in one hand, and with the other hand, twist the pipe cleaner ends together under the chin. The hair-do will cover up the bit of pipe cleaner that is over the head.

Hair

A lock of wool is a part of a fleece as it was sheared from a sheep. A lock that has not been carded retains its natural curl and luster. Various breeds of sheep have different curl, so the options are endless.

While the glue gun is warming up, organize the locks of wool you plan to use.

Place a dab of glue on the pipe cleaner at the top of the head and apply the first lock to cover it. Continue adding more hair until you are satisfied with the style.

Attach the head

Snip a small hole in the dress at the top center of the fold. It should be just large enough to slip the pipe cleaner ends through.

Slip the pipe cleaner head assembly, feet first, into the dress through the top center slit.

Lift the dress up, then take a second pipe cleaner and wrap it crosswise around the head assembly, so that the ends extend out of the sleeves. Trim the pipe cleaners so they protrude from each sleeve about 1 inch. These will be the hands.

Fold the dress back down and use the glue gun to seal up the sides.

Thread a bell through each hand and secure it by twisting the pipe cleaner around the bell and tucking the end into the sleeve.

For the hanger, cut a 12-inch piece of ribbon and tie an end around each hand. Trim the ends, and she is finished.

DESIGN TIPS:

Create a window valance with several angels by twisting their hands together.

Create an angel in the likeness of someone you know.

Do an international series, creating different dresses from around the world.

Persian Muq Ruq

*T*his intricate design begins in a geometric framework of multiple borders that you establish with a ruler. You will begin modifying some complicated woven motifs into simple shapes to create a miniature Persian rug.

Materials

Wool

White pre-felt
Various colors of carded wool. For this rug I used Harrisville Designs fiber in Blue-grass, Russet, Tundra, Seagreen, Lime, Hemlock, and Adobe.
Pencil roving in Turquoise and Orange

Felting Needle

38 triangular

DESIGN TIP:

Background Geometry
Middle Eastern rug designs were the inspiration for several projects in this book.

Get your feet wet with some new design ideas by leafing through a book of these beautiful woven (or knotted) rugs. You can't help but notice that they have multiple borders that take up a good portion of the design space and allow for many opportunities to play with color and design.

Cut a piece of pre-felt that measures 6 x 8 inches. Use a ruler and a permanent marker to draw a 5 x 7-inch rectangle.

The extra inch around the outside will not have any design on it but is great to leave for a final border and scissor trimming after the wet felting has been done.

The entire design area will be needled, so you can make a mistake with your permanent marker without affecting the end result.

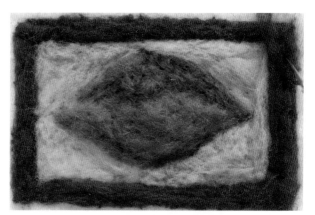

The background geometry is groundwork for the details which will be needled on top of the base colors. Choose colors for the background that will provide some contrast; this example alternated between dark and light colors. Follow along with this example or create your own design.

Needle the background colors down tightly. Use a straight up and down poking motion. The work of the needle is being done on the bottom inch where the barbs are located. The needle must penetrate the pre-felt and land well into the needling board underneath. Remember, in order to prevent the needle from snapping, pull it from the needling board at the same angle it was inserted.

Outline each change of color. Pencil roving works great for this task as it provides a consistent fine line and is easy to work with. It is also an opportunity to add more color, which enhances the overall detail.

To create a medallion, start in the center with a dab of wool and create a dot by poking the wool repeatedly in the same area. Pull the needle all the way out and poke again and again in the same spot. Build outward from the center dot with evenly spaced petals.

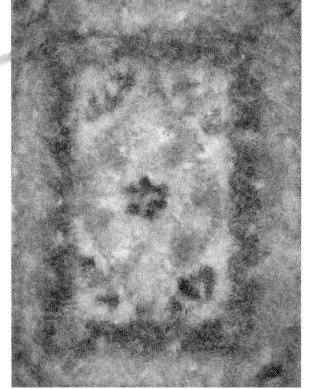

You will notice that your rug adheres to the needling board. Rotate it frequently by gently lifting it up. Pulling too hard at one corner may distort your pre-felt base. If this occurs, tug it gently back into shape before continuing.

Working with small designs can be challenging. Use wisps of fiber to create details and add more if needed. You will be amazed at what a tiny dab of fiber can look like on the felt.

Create detail within each background color. Simple shapes and color changes can look dynamic. Petals, vines, and medallions are easy shapes to create and look intricate. Use a sunrise or starburst design to brighten up the corners.

Needle the design thoroughly to prepare it for wet felting. The photo at bottom right illustrates the back of the design. It was needled so tightly that the original pre-felt color is barely discernible. The more you are able to needle, the less migration of fiber you will have during the wet felting stage. It is especially important on this project, as there are many small details.

Set up a wet felting area according to the instructions in the beginning of the book.

Lay the rug face down on the plastic. By laying it face down, you will tighten the back fibers first and minimize the amount of fiber migrating to the front.

Fill a bowl with a few cups of hot tap water, scrunch a plastic grocery bag in your fist, and dip it in the water. Keep the bowl next to your felt. Press the wet bag down on the rug, pushing the water into the pre-felt. Continue until the pre-felt is saturated and water pools around your fingers when you press down.

Put soap on the palm of your hand and glide it over the surface in a circular or back and forth motion, gently at first then more aggressively. The continuous motion of your hand is agitating the fibers and tightening the fabric, creating felt. When your hand stops gliding smoothly, add more soap. Your pre-felt will shrink during the wet felt process as the fibers entangle. To be sure it maintains its shape, keep the rug flat and use an even amount of pressure in all areas, checking periodically with a ruler. If one area shrinks more and distorts the shape, try applying extra agitation to the opposite area to bring it back in line.

Continue wet felting until the piece has tightened and shrunk down to approximately 5½ x 7 inches. The amount it shrinks depends on the variables discussed at the beginning of the book, including how forcefully you agitate it and for how long. The measurements are merely guidelines—a little smaller or larger is fine.

Rinse the rug thoroughly to remove the soap, and use a hot iron on both sides of the rug to flatten and smooth the fibers. Place a cloth between the iron and the felt in order to prevent burning and to absorb some of the moisture. It is never too late to touch it up with the needles if needed. Lay the rug flat to dry, then trim the edges with scissors.

If the rug has become distorted after the wet felting is complete, try reshaping it by tugging gently while it is wet. This will work for small tweaks and alignments, but because of the elasticity in wool, you may need to saturate it again with hot soapy water and felt it some more.

To clean your rug, wash by hand in warm soapy water.

Elegant Persian designs

Bear Mug Rug

*T*his project shows you how to create a three-dimensional form that adds a new depth to your needling skills. It introduces the STAR needle, and if you choose, it will also introduce you to combed fiber. Once you have learned how to make this simple bear, you can use the same design principles to create other animals.

Materials

Wool

Black pre-felt (body)
Ashland Bay Colonial TOP in Black
  (combed fiber for the head)
Pelsau Wool in Ochre (carded fiber for the
  snout, facial features, and claws)
Small dab of any white wool

Felting Needles

38 triangular
Star needle

Finishing

Sewing needle and black thread

The bear is done in two parts. The body is flat and the head is done as a three dimensional shape. They are attached together with a needle and thread once both are complete.

Body

Use two layers of pre-felt for the body. Trace the stencil located in the back of the book on the pre-felt with a permanent marker. Cut the bodies out. The stencil for this project was 11 inches long; the prefelt for the body started at 11 inches. If you see some of the permanent marker lines, turn it over and use the other side.

Place the two layers together on the needling board.

Needle three claws on each paw using a small amount of Ochre fiber. You will use this color again on the face of the bear. Use a straight up and down motion to poke the wool through.

The work of the needle is being done on the bottom inch where the barbs are located. Push the fiber down with the needle, penetrating the pre-felt and landing in the needling board. The barbs are pushing some of the strands of fiber through, forcing entanglement. Inserting the needle at an angle is a great way to adjust the placement of fiber, but be sure to pull it out at the same angle to prevent the needle from snapping.

Because there is so little needling on the bear's body, it is important to needle the two layers of pre-felt together before you begin to wet felt, otherwise the two layers may not felt together. Needle the edges together all the way around with a few taps, and then needle the entire body. A multi-needled tool helps get the job done quickly.

Wet felt the body gently to maintain the original shape and proportions. You don't need to obtain any great shrinkage, just wet felt it long enough for the two layers to secure together and the claw fibers to felt to the body.

Set up a wet felting area according to the instructions in the beginning of the book. Cradle the bear's pelt in your hands and run it under the tap, saturating it with hot water. Lay it on top of the plastic. Press it gently to be sure that the water pools around your fingers in all areas.

Put soap on the palm of your hand to act as a lubricant, allowing your hand to glide smoothly over the surface. The continuous motion of your hand is agitating the fiber and making felt. Add more soap as needed. You will see and feel the fibers tighten and shrink, creating a dense fabric—felt. Agitate each side gently for about ten minutes, maintaining the proportions of the body.

Rinse the felt thoroughly to remove the soap. Use a hot iron to flatten and smooth the body. Be sure to place a cloth between the iron and the felt to prevent burning and to absorb some of the moisture. Trim the edges into shape with scissors if needed. Lay the body flat to dry. Set it aside until you have completed the head of the bear.

Head

In this half of the project, you will be creating three-dimensional felt using a felting needle with a star configuration.

Look closely at the bottom inch of a variety of felting needles to see how the barbs are configured differently. The best way to learn about the variety in the needles is by trying them. The wrong needle will struggle to penetrate the wool and could cause hand strain. It also may not push enough fiber through for the task, causing you to do unnecessary repetitive poking.

The star configuration tends to push more fiber and works well for firming rounded shapes more quickly than a needle with a triangular configuration.

This project is demonstrated in combed fiber but could easily be done with carded fiber. While combed fiber is challenging to use in needling tapestry designs and requires more instruction for wet felting, it is great for rolling the three-dimensional heads, providing a smoother surface with more luster.

To prevent poking yourself, avoid distractions and always poke straight down toward the needling board.

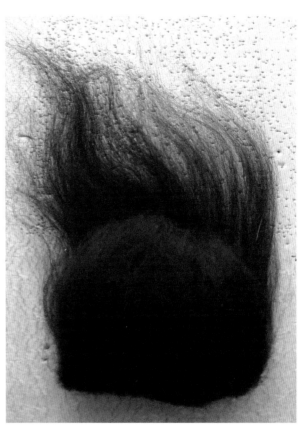

Use black combed or carded wool and begin by rolling the fiber tightly into a ball, tapping it with the needles as you roll to secure it, until it is about 5 inches around. Secure the end fibers with the needle.

It is important to always be needling down toward the needling board and to lay the board flat on top of a table. This is especially important when creating a multi-dimensional shape.

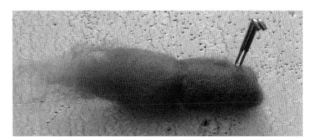

To create the snout, use the same Ochre carded fiber you used for the claws. Roll the fiber about 2 inches wide, tapping one half of it with the needles as you roll it and leaving 1 inch free of needling. This loose end is where the snout will be attached to the head. Roll the fiber until your snout is about 2 inches around.

Watch your fingers—they will be holding and rolling the fiber and may be very close to the needle tips!

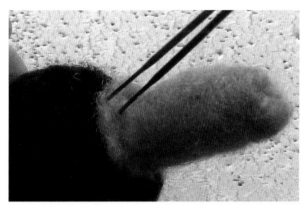

Needle the fluffy end of the snout to the head, moving the needles all the way around the circumference of the snout until it is securely attached.

Poke straight down into the snout to adjust the length as it protrudes from the face. You want it to be about 1 inch long. It will shorten some more when you needle the nose and mouth.

Wrap some more black fiber over the seam where the two colors meet and needle it down. This will clean up the needling join.

Needle the head all over to tighten the fibers and prepare the surface for the facial details. This is a chance to make corrections in the shape of the head, which should still be round.

Use carded fiber for the facial features. It is challenging to use combed fiber to needle small details.

Use the same color as the snout to create the eyes. Needle a circle and an eyebrow above it. Use black carded fiber to make a small dot inside the eye for the pupil.

Use an even smaller dab of white fiber to make a twinkle in each eye. Because it is such a small amount of fiber, you will need to poke the fiber in the same spot repeatedly. Place the sparkle in approximately the same spot on each eye.

To create a nose, first use carded black fiber and needle a line from top to bottom on the end of the snout; use the center of the eyes to line it up. Needle a nose on the snout in the shape of

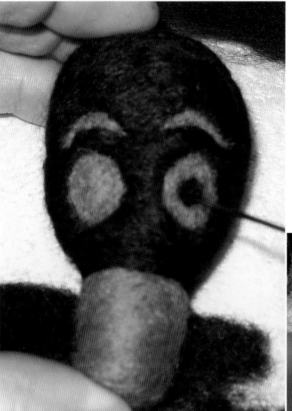

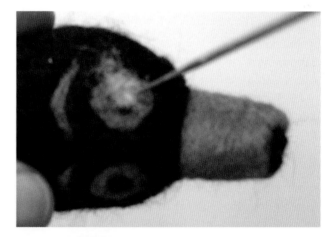

Constructing the head

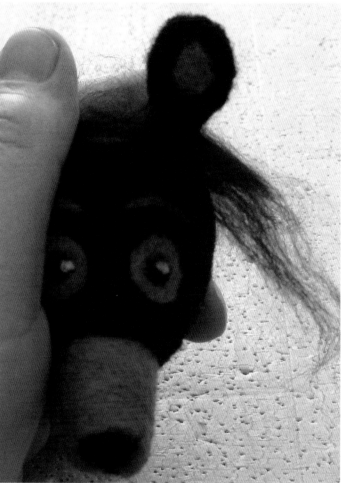

an upside-down triangle. For the mouth, needle another line of black carded fiber that extends from one side of the snout to the other.

For the ears, begin with a wispy tuft of black fiber about 4 inches long, 1 inch thick, and 1 inch wide. Fold the tuft in half and pinch the ends together. Needle the remaining top inch of fiber into a circular shape a bit smaller than the size of a dime. The extra fiber that you are pinching on the bottom will be used to attach the ear to the head. Make two the same size. Use the same color wool as the snout to needle a dab of fiber inside the ears—it gives nice depth and makes him look like a teddy bear.

Spread out the loose strands of fiber over the bear's crown, and then needle them all the way around the head, securing the ear tightly. Position the second ear on the head, symmetrically balanced with the first one, and needle all over to secure any loose fibers.

Trim any stray fibers with scissors. Lay the body down and place the head on top to line it up. Use a sewing needle and black thread to attach the head to the body with a few stitches.

The next project, a dragon table centerpiece, will illustrate how to make teeth and horns, and you could use the same techniques to create antlers or different snouts, all made by simply needling in different areas.

The natural lanolin in wool creates a water-resistant barrier, perfect for your new mug rug.

Dragon Table Centerpiece

This is another project involving a three-dimensional form. It will also introduce you to some new design shapes to make your animals more elaborate, including teeth, horns, and various shapes to enhance the design of your dragon.

Materials

Wool

White pre-felt
Carded wool fiber in any color combination

Felting Needles

38 triangular
Star needle

Finishing

Sewing needle and thread

This project is done in two parts. The body is needle felted flat and the head is done as a three dimensional form. They are attached together with a needle and thread once they are complete.

Body

Enlarge the stencil in this book to accommodate any size body that you like. This example used a body that was 14 inches long.

Use two layers of pre-felt and trace around the stencil with a permanent marker. To lend durability and depth to the dragon, you will be needling through both layers.

Remove the stencil and draw in the leg areas. Don't worry about copying the stencil or drawing in all of the details—the shapes and designs that you create might be more interesting! The entire design area will be needled, so you can make a mistake with your permanent marker without affecting the end result.

HELPFUL HINT:

Another way to transfer a design to the pre-felt is by taping the stencil to a window and taping one layer of pre-felt over it. Use the natural light to trace the design. Add the other layer of pre-felt under it when you start the needling.

Lay the body on top of the needling board so that your needle has a place to land as it penetrates the pre-felt.

Think about what color you will use for the head of your dragon. Since that will be the main color, you can create balance by using that color now in the body. Be flexible and creative about changing design and color combinations as you go along—play around with colors until you find the right combination.

Begin anywhere—follow along with this design or create your own style!

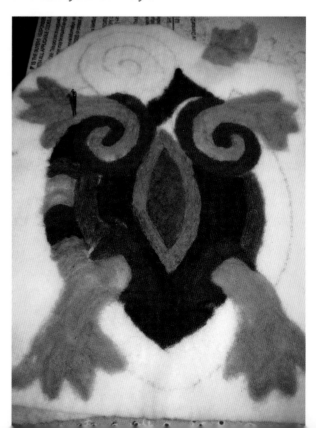

Needle the wool down using a straight up and down poking motion, gently at first until you are sure about the placement of each color, then needle the design tightly. If you change your mind, you can always needle over a color. Don't try to pull out fiber that has been needled securely as it may distort the pre-felt base.

Join the colors right up against one another as you add them.

You will notice the pre-felt adhering to the needling board. Rotate it frequently by gently lifting it up off the board. If the pre-felt becomes distorted, tug it gently back into shape before you continue needling.

Outline all the color changes in black to provide extra contrast. This technique really makes the design stand out.

The nails are simple almond shapes needled on the top of each toe. The black outlining highlights the details. Needle a few strands between the almond nails to create a more distinct toe.

Is it needled enough? Run your hand over the surface to check for shifting fibers and needle down any loose or stray strands. Flip the body over—the design should be clearly distinguishable on the backside. A character this cute is sure to be handled often so make it more durable by wet felting it.

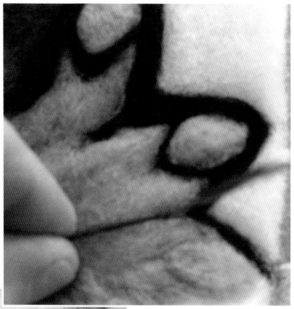

Needled surfaces, front and back

Set up a wet felting area according to the instructions in the beginning of the book.

HELPFUL HINT:

As the projects progress, they increase in size, and you should consider using other tools to help during wet felting. Using your hand to create all the agitation is fine for small projects but time consuming and hard on your hands as the pieces get larger. The wet felting section at the beginning of the book gives you ideas for tools you could use to make the wet felting process more efficient.

Lay the dragon's body face down on the plastic. By felting the back first, you will minimize the possible migration of fibers to the front.

Fill a bowl with a few cups of hot water and keep it next to your felt. Scrunch up a plastic grocery bag in your fist and submerge it in the hot water, then place the bag over the dragon. Press down, releasing the trapped water onto the pre-felt. The lanolin in wool is naturally resistant to water, so pressing it helps the saturation process.

You are ready to begin the agitation when you press down and water pools around your fingers in all areas. Put some soap on the palm of your hand and glide it over the surface. Begin agitating gently and become gradually more aggressive.

The soap acts as a lubricant, allowing your hand to glide smoothly over the surface of the wet pre-felt. The continuous motion of your hand is forcing entanglement of fibers, making felt. Add more hot water or soap as needed to keep your hand gliding smoothly. You will begin to see and feel the fibers tighten and shrink, creating a dense fabric. The amount it shrinks depends on how much you continue to rub. Agitate each side aggressively for about fifteen minutes.

A washboard will make the wet felting process happen quickly. Once you have spent a few minutes agitating it with your hand and you are able to handle the wet fabric, place it on top of the washboard. Run some extra water over it and add some more soap. Gently glide the felt over the ridges of the board, becoming more aggressive as it tightens.

When using a washboard, it is important to move the felt frequently, changing the direction of the agitation and working each area of the felt evenly to avoid shrinking it too much in one place, which will cause distortion. Add more soap as needed to keep it gliding smoothly.

If you don't use a washboard, continue with your hand until you feel the fibers have tightened and shrunk about 1 inch. Keep an eye on the original shape and proportions as you wet felt. You don't need to shrink the body much, simply wet felt it long enough for the fibers to tighten together.

Rinse the body thoroughly to remove the soap and use a hot iron to smooth the felt fabric. Put a cloth between the felt and the iron to prevent burning and to absorb some of the moisture.

If the felt has become distorted after the wet felting is complete, try reshaping it by tugging gently while it is wet. You could also wet it out again and felt it some more.

If your design was not needled securely and fibers have shifted, you can always touch it up with more needling.

Once it is dry, shave the surface if needed with a disposable razor and use a lint roller to clean up any loose fibers. Trim the edges all the way around and set the body aside until the head is complete.

Flat dragon body completed

Head

When creating a multi-dimensional shape, it is important to always be needling down toward the needling board and to lay the board flat on top of a table.

To maintain a balance of color between the body and the head, use the same color choices for each part. This head will be worked with carded fiber in the same color as the legs.

A needle with a star configuration is preferable for three dimensional needling because it pushes more fiber at once and gets the job done quicker than a needle with a triangular configuration.

Roll the fiber up tightly into the size and shape of a jumbo egg. Secure the fibers as you roll, tapping the fiber with the needles until the head is about 7 inches around. Secure the end fibers with a few taps of the needle and set the egg aside.

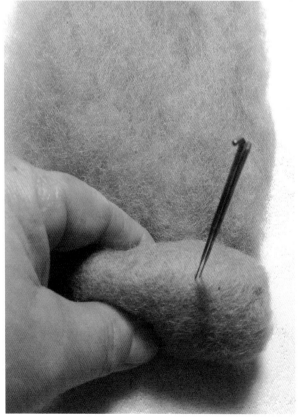

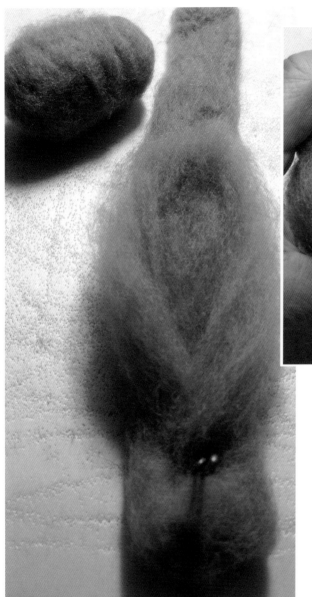

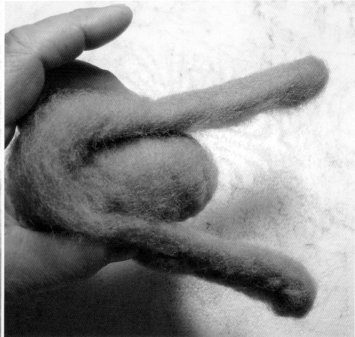

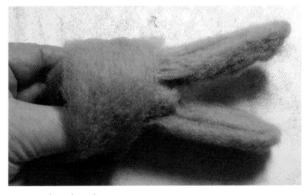

Dragon head underway

To create the jaw, begin with a piece of carded fiber 4 inches wide, 12 inches long, and about 1 inch thick.

Needle the two ends about 4 inches on top and bottom, leaving the 4 inches of fiber in the middle free of needling. That is where you will secure the jaw to the head.

Fold the edges in toward the center as you needle until it is about 1 inch wide. Flip it and do the same on the other end. One end will be the upper jaw and the other is the bottom jaw.

Wrap the jaw around the egg-shaped head and secure them together where the fiber is still fluffy. The top and the bottom of the jaw should each be approximately 4 inches long, 1 inch wide, and

1 inch thick. Needle in more fiber if needed. As you begin needling the details, the tighter and smaller the head will become.

Wrap some fiber around the entire jaw assembly to cover up any seams and needle it securely.

Fill the entire inside of the mouth with black fiber. Try not to poke the fiber all the way through the upper and lower jaw, as black strands will appear on the outside. Needle them down just far enough to be secured. Tighten the entire head by needling all the way around. Next you will begin to add the facial details.

The tongue can be any color you like. Start with a piece of carded fiber about 4 inches long, 1 inch wide, and 1 inch high. Leave ½ inch at

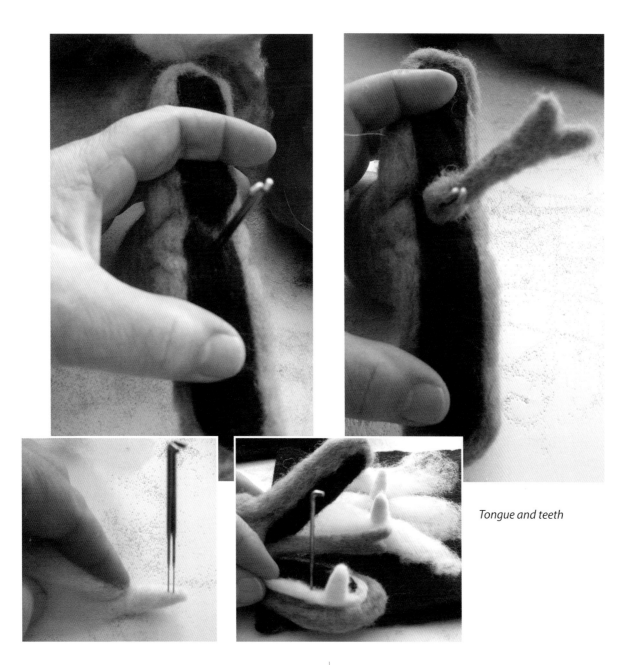

Tongue and teeth

one end fluffy—this will be used to secure the tongue to the head. Separate the other end in two to create a forked tongue. Roll it and rotate it frequently as you needle it into shape.

Secure the tongue in the back of the throat by poking in the same area repeatedly. When the loose fibers are all needled in, give it a tug to be sure it is secure.

Trim any loose or stray fibers with a pair of small, sharp scissors.

For the teeth, use a piece of white carded fiber about 3 inches long, 1 inch wide, and 1 inch high. Make a triangular shape with your fingers by pinching one end. Each tooth will be a cone shape, and you can create this by rolling

it as you tap it with the needles; continue rolling it and tapping it, pulling the fiber into the center and needling the tip more to create the conical shape.

Leave about 1½ inches at one end fluffy so that you can attach the tooth to the mouth.

Watch out for your fingers! When needling this small and close, it is important to pay attention to where your needles are landing.

Make four teeth—two for the upper jaw and two for the lower. Of course, you can make your dragon as toothy as you like!

Once the fiber is cone shaped, trim any stray fibers with a small pair of scissors, but don't cut off the fluffy end.

Spread the fluffy end of the tooth out, separating it into two sections. Put the first tooth in the mouth, spread the fluffy white wool on either side of the tooth into a line, and needle it down. This trick will give the impression of more teeth in the mouth. Do the same on the other side. Flip the head over and attach the other two teeth, always needling downward toward the board.

For the eyeballs, roll white wool into two balls, each about 1 inch around. Determine the location of the first eyeball on the side of the head and tap it into place by slipping the needles under the ball and needling into the same spot repeatedly. Tap evenly on the outside of the eye, moving the needles around the circumference of the white wool until it is firm but still protrudes from the head. Attach the other eye on the opposite side of the head.

Next, make two eyelids. Use a chunk of fiber 1 inch thick, 1 inch wide, and 1½ inches long, leaving ½ inch on the end fluffy to secure them to the head. Needle the top into an oval by rolling the edges into the center; flip them over and needle from both sides until they are firm. Trim any extra fibers with scissors. Secure the

Eyes and eyelids

Constructing the fancy comb

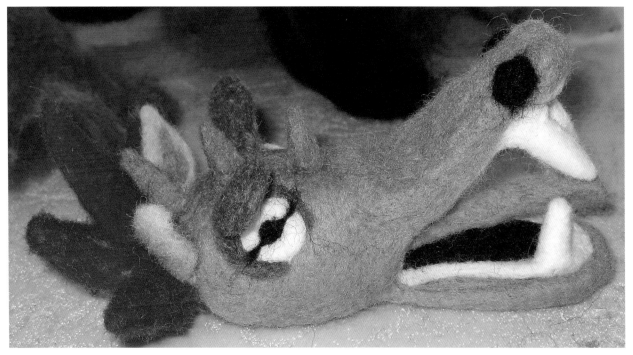

fluffy ends to the top of the eyeballs by separating the end in two as you did for the teeth and carrying the fiber around the edge, outlining the eye while securing the lid.

Create a comb for his head by using a piece of carded fiber about 4 inches wide, 4 inches long, and 1 inch high. Separate the top into four distinct points. Needle this by rolling the edges in toward the center of each point, flipping it over often and needling from both sides until it is firm. Remember to leave the end fluffy to secure it to the head.

Line up the comb before needling it securely into place. Attach it to the head by needling the fluffy part. Create a point when securing it, and it will blend nicely into the design on the body.

The ears are a simple almond shape, or they can be oval if you prefer. Add a bit of another color for the inside. Remember to always leave one end of the fiber fluffy to attach it to the head.

For the horns, choose a color that you used in the body to maintain balance. Leave the bottom ¼ inch fluffy and make a conical shape, just like the teeth. Make as many as you like, small or large.

Use black wool for the nostrils and tap it into two oval shapes, one on each side of the snout.

Fill in the pupil center and add a small dab of fiber going straight across or up and down.

Line up the head with the body and use a needle and thread to make a few stitches underneath to sew them together.

DESIGN TIP:

There are many variations for this design that you can try to give your dragon different looks. In this example, I used an almond-shaped eye to make him fierce and more reptilian. I also love the flowing mane; the strands were created using the same needling technique used for making the teeth.

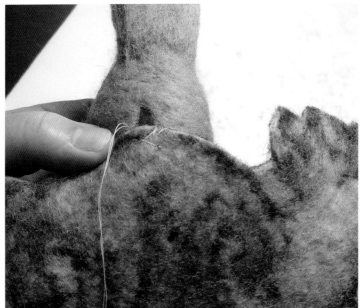

Putting the dragon together

Portraiture

*H*uman faces share certain geometric similarities that make it easy to get started in portraiture!

In this project, you will learn the geometry of the face and some new shading techniques. If you don't have a patient model that is willing to sit for you, try using a photograph instead. It is helpful if your model is looking straight toward you (or the camera) for your first portrait, as it will help you learn the basic geometric alignments of the face.

Materials

Wool

White pre-felt
White, black, gray, flesh tones, and any other colors needed for the skin tone of your model

Felting Needle

38 triangular

Finishing

A frame with a mat board opening of 8½ x 11½ inches
Sewing needle and thread
Mat board

HELPFUL HINT:

No wet felting needed for this project!

Cut two pieces of pre-felt measuring 14 x 17 inches. The size will allow plenty of room for framing, and the double layer of pre-felt will add strength when you stretch it for framing. Pre-felt is thin and fragile, so you will be needling through both layers.

Try using a needling board that is the size of the pre-felt. The insulation board described in the beginning of the book provides a firm resistance and will allow you to rest your wrist on the surface as you work. Remember to lift your pre-felt gently off the needling board as you progress.

Because the background will have no needling and light colors are used, you won't be drawing anything on the pre-felt base. This entire project will be freestyle—you CAN do it just by following some simple guidelines.

In the center of the pre-felt, use a flesh-toned wool to create an egg or oval shape approximately 5 inches wide by 7 inches tall and slightly narrowing at the bottom where the chin will be.

This will be the head, and all the facial details will be needled on top. Use a straight up and down poking motion, inserting the needle about 1 inch through the pre-felt and landing well into the needling board underneath.

With white, create two almond-shaped eyes in the center of the head, spacing them one eye length apart. Add a line that will be the base of the mouth. The corners of the mouth should be in line with the center of the eyes.

The nostrils line up approximately with the tear ducts at the inner corners of the eyes. At this stage you are lining up the proportions—the geometry that we all share—and creating the groundwork. The details will follow.

Start filling in the hair, trying to get the shape correct as it relates to the rest of the head. Don't worry about the exact color—that will be added later—just get the correct proportions. How long are the bangs? Do they cover the eyebrows? Do you see the ears, or is the hair covering them?

The ears begin at eye level and extend to the bottom of the nose. Are your model's ears close to the head, or do they stick out?

The best advice seems like the simplest and the most obvious—paint (with wool) what you see.

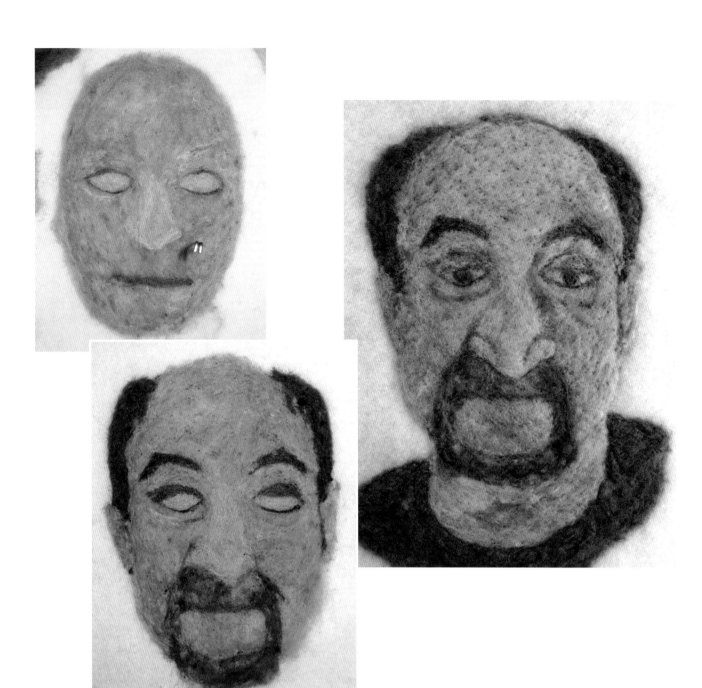

Blending and Layering

There are so many variations in skin tones it is difficult to match every one with wool. If you have a limited range of wool colors, many shades can be created with some simple techniques.

Blend small amounts of fiber with your fingertips by holding two colors together and pulling them simultaneously using both hands, bringing them together and pulling them apart again, and repeating that motion over and over until you have the color you need. This is a great technique if you need only a small dab of a certain color.

You can create new colors or change the value of a color by adding lighter or darker colors. For example, start with a flesh tone and add white to make a lighter tint; or add black, dark red, or deep orange to make a darker hue. Change the tone by adding gray or even a bit of green.

Wisp a few strands of fiber over the foundation color to create many different shades. Layering color adds dimension to your portrait—after all, our complexions have many different shades that create our individual skin tone.

More flesh tone added to the lower portion of the original egg shape creates a broader jaw.

Consider the unique characteristics of your model. Does he have a broad jaw or a thin face, a crooked nose or a tiny one? Are her eyes close set, does she have a small chin or a pronounced one, a small mouth or full lips? How about facial hair, moles, wrinkles on the forehead, high cheekbones, ruddy cheeks, or bags under the eyes? Note that the arch and thickness of the eyebrows are different for everyone. Thinking about all of these details as you progress will help you create a solid foundation.

Use a darker shade of flesh tone for the eyelids; you will lighten them later by needling a few strands of a lighter-toned fiber on top of the dark.

Look at the area where the nose attaches to the face and try to mimic your model to create the shading at that connection. You may need to make a few attempts. This can be the trickiest part, and the best advice I can give you is to not give up—keep working it, keep experimenting, and know that errors are easily fixed.

If you feel as though you have botched the nose and need a "clean slate," cover it over with the original flesh color and begin again! It will come to you.

Remember, the nuances in skin tone create texture and add dimension to your portrait. Use a darker flesh tone to create wrinkles, eyelids, and bags under the eyes. A few wispy strands can create great effect in revealing age.

When adding the neck, whether you have a live model or a picture, look at where the neck attaches to the head in relation to the jaw. This connection will be different depending on the posture and stance of your model. Again, paint with the wool exactly what you see. Continue working the details, a little here and a little there. Eventually your model will begin to emerge.

To match gray hair, wisp white over a darker color. Remember, every detail is easily adjusted or corrected!

Creating a sparkle in the eye will add life to your portrait! Needle in a black pupil and place a very small dab of white wool in the eye. Secure the tiny white dab by poking in the same spot repeatedly.

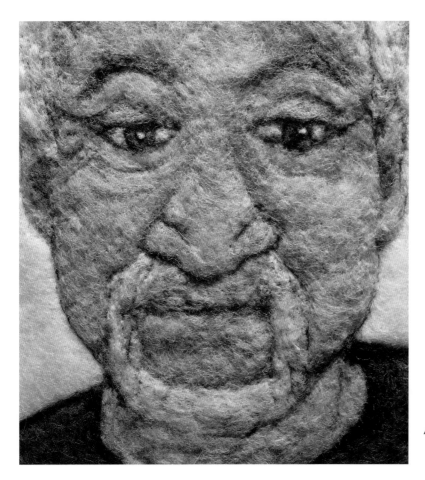

Adding detail brings a portrait to life

The more you play with the finishing stages, the better your portrait will be. Felt is a forgiving medium and changes may be easily made.

With a few wispy strands of black wool, barely outline the head so that it stands out from the white pre-felt background.

Since this project is not wet felted, needle the portrait tightly. Place a damp cloth over the finished portrait and with a hot iron press it on both sides. The steam created by the iron will help smooth out the surface of the felt, erasing the marks made by the needle, and will flatten and secure the fibers in the back.

Framing Your Portrait

The dimensions of this portrait fit well with a mat opening of $8\frac{1}{2}$ x $11\frac{1}{2}$ inches.

Center the wool felt on the mat board. The mat board should be smaller than the frame size to accommodate the thickness of the wool.

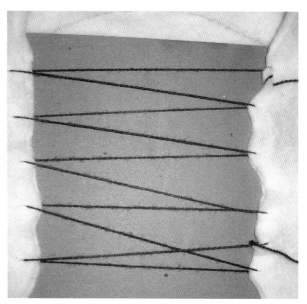

Fold the edges to the back and use any fine yarn or thread to stitch across the back from side to side and top to bottom. It should be taut, but not so tight as to pucker the board. As you work, check the front often to be sure it is centered.

Heat and humidity may cause wool to sweat under glass, so if you frame this portrait, use a frame with no glass.

Maple Leaf Coaster

In this easy project you will learn to create felt from carded wool. In the previous projects you used a machine made pre-felt as your base; however, in this project you will learn to make your own pre-felt.

Materials

Wool

Carded wool in colors of your choice—about 1½ ounces for each leaf. I used Harrisville Designs carded fiber in Marigold, Russet, Poppy, Melon, and Foliage.

Felting Needle

38 triangular

As you have seen, wet felting is a simple process involving hot water, soap, and agitation. Wool fibers have microscopic barb-like scales that entangle and interlock when subjected to pressure, moisture, and agitation resulting in a dense and durable fabric.

To ensure success as a beginner, the wool you select should be:

- From the same mill blend or from the same breed of sheep. Each breed of sheep produces wool that has a different scale structure, and they do not always felt well together.
- Carded, not combed, fiber. When wool is combed (also called TOP) it has been prepared so that the strands of fibers are running parallel to each other, and it requires special techniques for wet felting. When wool is carded, the fibers are bent and lay in a disorganized fashion, allowing the strands of fiber to interlock more easily. Carded fiber is much easier to work with, especially for beginners.

Set up a wet felting work station according to the instructions in the beginning of the book.

As you progress through the book, the projects increase in size and complexity. This project will demonstrate some of the tools that make the wet felting process happen more quickly and are especially useful as you move forward.

Build a circular mound of fiber on top of the plastic by laying out any combination of reds, oranges, and yellows that pleases you. The circle should be about 13 inches wide and 1 inch thick. Make the ends of each color wisp out as you lay them down—this will help the fibers lock together by allowing them to entangle more easily.

During the agitation, the scales are hooking onto one another and being forced to entangle as you apply pressure. If the wool is layered in thick chunks, it will be more difficult for the strands to attach properly to other fibers, which could cause weak areas or holes in the finished felt fabric. If you end up with some weak spots, don't worry, we can correct them in the needling stage. It's a fun learning experience, and nearly every error can be remedied!

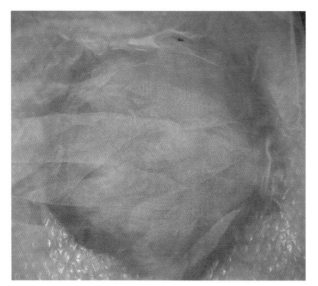

Cover the wool with a piece of sheer nylon curtain material and press your hand on the surface to make sure all areas feel evenly thick. If you feel a weak area, lift the curtain and add more wool to that spot.

The curtain is essential when beginning to wet felt raw wool. It restricts the movement of the fibers as you saturate them with hot water and will allow you to begin agitation without disturbing the mound of carded wool. Your hand, lathered in soap, will glide over the surface of the curtain, leaving the wool intact.

It is important to leave the mound flat on the plastic until it is partially felted. If you attempt to pick it up before you have begun the agitation, it will fall apart.

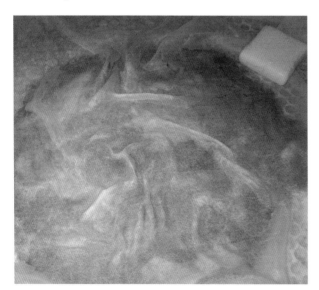

Fill a bowl with a few cups of hot water and keep it next to your felt. Scrunch up a plastic grocery bag in your fist and submerge it in the

hot water, then place the bag over the mound of fiber and press down, releasing the trapped water onto the curtain-covered wool. Repeat this process until the entire piece is saturated. Check by pressing on the mound in all areas to be certain that the water pools around your fingers.

Put some soap on the palm of your hand and glide it over the surface. Begin gently, with a light hand. Add more soap to your palm as needed. The soap acts as a lubricant, allowing your hand to glide smoothly over the surface of the curtain.

At this stage, if you notice a weak area or a hole you will not be able to add any more wool; just keep going and you can fix it later. Remove the curtain after a couple of minutes and continue with the hand felting.

. . . .

The curtain should be removed as soon as possible. Fibers may migrate through the surface of the nylon and lock on top, felting the nylon to the wool. If you see the fibers begin to migrate through the surface of the curtain, remove it and continue felting with your hand.

. . . .

Use a gentle hand at first, gliding over the surface in a circular or back and forth motion. Gradually become more aggressive, adding more soap as needed to keep your hand moving smoothly. The agitation you create with the continuous movement is turning the wool to felt.

Work the entire surface until you see and feel the fibers tighten and shrink; you may apply more pressure as the fibers begin to tighten. Pushing out a little excess water here and there can help the felting process. If there is too much water, the strands of fibers may swim right past each other and not have a chance to become entangled. Not having enough water can also impede the process, so be sure it is saturated and add more hot water anytime it is needed.

Wet felting this project will take a little extra time, since you started with raw wool. You will also experience more shrinkage than the previous projects where you lent structure to the fabric by needling it. Stop wet felting when the circle measures about 11 inches in diameter. You have made your own pre-felt! The leaf will be wet felted again after the trimming and needling, so the fibers will tighten even more.

Rinse the piece of felt thoroughly to remove the soap. Press with a hot iron on both sides, placing a cloth between the felt and the iron to prevent burning and to absorb some of the moisture. Lay the felt flat to dry.

Trace the leaf stencil found in the back of this book on the felt with a permanent marker and cut it out. This is the time to strengthen any weak areas, fill in any holes, or add a new splash of color by needling wool where needed or desired.

The next step is to needle in the leaf veins. Choose a darker shade of red to create some contrast.

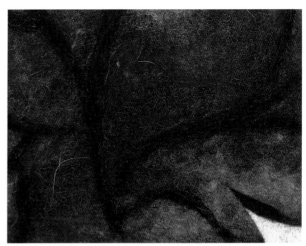

Start with three major lines beginning from the base of the stem to the tip of each section; the smaller veins will branch out from them. Needle as many or as few as you like. Use prepared pencil roving to create even lines or use a section of carded fiber the approximate diameter of a pencil.

Secure the veins and any color additions by wet felting the leaf again. This will tighten all the fibers together and create a dense fabric. You could expect another inch of shrinkage, ending up with a leaf that measures about 10 inches from the tip of the leaf to the end of the stem.

The second wet felting will cause the crisp edges to become a little fuzzy, so trim them if you like.

To clean your leaf, wash by hand in warm soapy water.

Other Wet Felting Tools

When you can handle the wool as a piece of fabric, you could use a washboard to finish the job quickly. The ridges provide an excellent surface for felting. Be sure you always have enough soap and water to keep the felt moving freely. Wool will shrink quickly when it is subjected to the ridges of a washboard, so stop to check your progress frequently.

Another handy tool for firming up your felt is a felt roller assembly. This tool keeps the wool flat on the textured mat as you felt. This is the most useful tool for the remaining projects in this book.

Check out the wet felting section at the beginning of the book to learn how to assemble a felt roller and for more information on wet felting techniques and other tools.

Dragon Table Runner

*T*his table runner has a couple of new techniques to challenge you.

The first is that you will be working with a single layer of pre-felt. As you have already experienced, pre-felt is a fragile material and should be handled gently until it is wet felted. The second challenge is working with a long piece of pre-felt while maintaining the desired symmetry, shape, and design.

Materials

Wool

Pre-felt, 15 x 70 inches. I used purple, but any dark color would work well.

Carded needling wool in fun colors to suit your taste. I used Harrisville Design fibers in Grass, Poppy, Fuchsia, Melon, Red, Goldenrod, Straw, White, Black, Seagreen, Black Cherry, Tundra, Lime, Marigold, Violet, and Scarlet.

Felting Needle

38 triangular

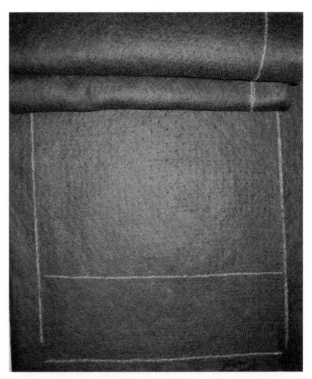

The pre-felt for this project is a single layer measuring 15 x 70 inches. Always start a bit larger than your desired dimensions to allow for the shrinkage that will occur during the wet felting.

With a permanent marker (metallic works best on dark pre-felt) and a yardstick, draw a line an inch in from the edge all the way around. This border will provide you with a little extra room for final trimming once the wet felting is complete. Now draw another line at each end, 5 inches in from the first line. Getting the background geometry drawn will give you a clear picture of the design space.

Place one end of the pre-felt on the needling board. Remember that the work of the needle is being done on the bottom inch where the barbs are located. Push the fiber down with the needle, penetrating the pre-felt and landing well into the needling board underneath. Use a straight up and down poking motion. The barbs on the bottom inch of the needle are pushing some strands of the carded wool through to the back. Inserting the needle at an angle is a great way to adjust the placement of fiber, but be sure to pull it out at the same angle to prevent the needle from snapping.

There is a negative space (the background) that will have no needling, so be sure not to draw any marks in that area.

Remember that because most pre-felt is fragile and can be torn or distorted easily, it is important to be gentle when lifting it off the needling board to rotate it.

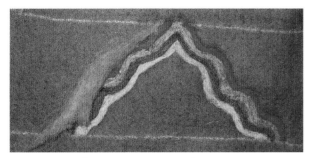

Needling fiber onto the pre-felt lends structure by adding density, creating a more durable surface to the single layer of pre-felt fabric. I chose a common Chinese textile design that filled up the entire 5-inch border at each end. It is a simple wavy pattern, but it looks complex with all the color changes.

Use a ruler to find the top center in each of the end borders. Start your first color there, and continue building on it. Make your color changing waves as wide or as narrow as you like; don't needle the design down tightly until you are certain of color and placement. The design space fills up fast!

Dragons are complex creatures, but designing one is simple—design a head, and the body will follow. Start at either end of the table runner and follow along with this design or create your own.

A dragon's body can be twisted in shapes that maximize the design space. Remember, simple shapes can look elaborate by the details added to them.

Fancy borders and details bring the dragon to life

Since dragons are mythical beasts they may take many shapes and colors. The suggestions shown are intended to get you started, but they leave lots of room for your own style and imagination.

The heads are simple shapes with lots of design flexibility. Enhance the design of your dragon by adding horns, teeth, a mane, or ears.

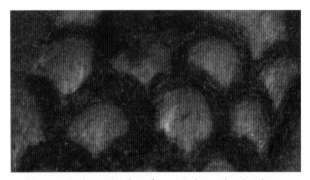

Use a darker shade of wool than the body to create the scales. Make a line of scallops or "U"

shapes, beginning anywhere. Add another line of scallops below it. Each row should be offset slightly so that the scales don't line up with the previous row.

Carded pencil roving is especially helpful for creating the scales. Pencil roving comes as a thin strand, approximately the diameter of a pencil. Because of the shape and preparation of the fiber, it is easy to needle (it takes less poking) and will give you even and consistent lines.

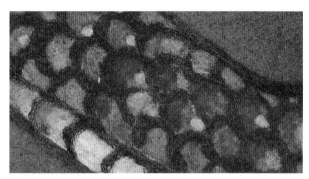

Add some color in the individual scales to create a gradient effect. It does not have to be in every scale, and the color used in each one may change. This technique is especially useful as the body twists and turns to accommodate the space available—you can add darker colors to create shadows and lighter ones for highlights. Outlining in black accents the design and really makes it pop.

A flowing mane was used here to show motion; it also allowed an opportunity to introduce a few colors from the border design.

An extra underbelly design breaks up the monotony of all the scales and allows another opportunity for some color changes.

There is a lot of red on this piece already, so to highlight the dragons' fiery breath, I introduced a bit of fuchsia on both ends. A new shade of orange, yellow, or even some purple would have looked nice too.

The tails meet in the center of the table runner, and compared to the colorful designs on each end, this area could look dull. I brightened it up and balanced the color by incorporating some of the end colors into the dragons' tails, adding yellow, some fuchsia, and a little orange.

Once the design is needled, your perfectly symmetrical outline may be slightly distorted. Gently stretch the pre-felt back into shape, using your yardstick to ensure straight edges. Needle a border color about ¼ inch wide all the way around to cover up the permanent marker lines and to frame the design.

FINAL FELTING

As the size of the projects increase, it becomes more difficult to wet felt with only your hand, and additional wet felting equipment is useful. Because of the size of this piece and the need to maintain the design's symmetry, a felt roller will serve well.

HELPFUL HINT:

Reference the wet felting section at the beginning of the book to learn how to make your own felt roller. It is a very useful tool for all stages of wet felting and is a great help when trying to maintain square edges.

If You Wet Felt by Hand

Fold the length of the runner in half with the design on the inside. Place plastic in between the two layers all the way to the fold so the two halves don't felt together. This is called a "resist." Tighten up the back fibers first. After you have saturated and worked the piece with some hand agitation, be sure to do the area where the felt is folded. Keep the plastic in between until you have done some hand felting on both sides of the table runner.

If You Wet Felt Using a Roller

Place the plastic on the towel with the textured surface side down and the needled table runner face down on top of the plastic. Once the runner is saturated, rest the PVC pipe at one end of the runner, then wrap the bubble wrap and the saturated felt together around the pipe and secure it. Roll it for 10 minutes or so, and then unroll the felt from the pipe. Roll the felt and bubble wrap on the pipe from the opposite end of the runner and roll for another 10 minutes. Continue switching from end to end and rolling, becoming more aggressive each time. Use your yardstick to be sure your edges are maintaining their squared shape. Continue this process until the table runner is sufficiently felted.

Prepare a wet felting space according to the instructions in the beginning of the book.

Fill a bowl with a few cups of hot water and keep it next to your felt. Scrunch up a plastic grocery bag in your fist and submerge it in the hot water, then place the bag over the table runner. Press down, releasing the trapped water onto the pre-felt. Repeat this process until the entire piece is saturated. The lanolin in wool is naturally resistant to water; using soap can help break through the surface of the fibers and assist the saturation process.

Water should pool around your fingers when you press down. Put soap on the palm of your hand and glide it over the surface, gently at first then more aggressively. The continuous movement of your hand is forcing the strands of fiber to entangle and tighten, creating felt. If your hand stops gliding smoothly, add more soap.

Your pre-felt will shrink during the wet felting process as the fibers tighten together. To be sure it maintains its shape, use an even amount of pressure in all areas, checking periodically with a yardstick. If one area shrinks more and the felt becomes distorted, try applying agitation to the opposite areas to bring it back into shape.

Apply more pressure as the fibers begin to tighten. Remember, pushing out a little excess water here and there can help the felting process. If there is too much water, the strands of fiber may swim right past each other and their scales will not have a chance to become entangled. Not having enough water can also impede the process and cause a roughened surface on your felt. Add more hot water as needed.

Keep a tape measure handy as you wet felt to measure your project as it shrinks and to be sure it retains square edges.

If you use a washboard to wet felt this project, use caution. With such a long piece of felt you must pay close attention to the dimensions to ensure that one side is not felting faster than the other.

Table Runner Tips

The most common problem when wet felting a piece this long is rippling edges. A table runner should lay flat on the table. Rippling occurs when more agitation and pressure are applied to the center of the piece than to the edges. If the edges of your piece ripple, try gently stretching it with your hands as you iron it; if the ripples are severe, you may need to wet it all over again, soap up, and use your hands to work just the edges.

Rinse the table runner thoroughly to remove the soap and press with a hot iron on both sides. Place a cloth between the iron and the felt to prevent burning and to absorb some of the excess water. Lay it flat to dry.

If you find the table runner is no longer squared at the corners, try stretching it into shape while it is wet. If it needs more than a little tweak, wet it again and felt the areas that need more attention, bringing it back to a rectangular shape. Wool has a lot of elasticity and stretches quite easily but may spring back into its original shape.

It is not too late to touch up the design with the needles if necessary.

Once it is dry, trim the edges square. The inch of pre-felt along the outside of the piece provides a small margin for trimming.

This table runner now measures 9 x 56 inches. The longer it is felted, the smaller it will get and the tighter the fabric becomes. The size of your finished piece may vary according to how aggressively you have felted it and for how long.

Medallion Pillow

By now you have acquired a lot of skill with the needles through the progression of projects in this book, and you have a basic understanding of the wet felting process. The next few projects will increase in size and complexity, providing you with some new challenges.

The following items are helpful for this project, as well as the remaining projects in this book:

- Multi-needled tools, especially for larger projects
- A needling board the size of your pre-felt
- A wet felting roller assembly is useful in maintaining squared edges and getting the wet felt done faster. Instructions on how to make your own roller are located at the beginning of the book.

Materials

Wool

White pre-felt
Carded wool in color combination of your
 choice

Felting Needle

38 triangular

Finishing

18-inch square pillow form
Coordinating fabric for the back of the pillow

The design process for this project begins with the background geometry. Once the stenciling is done and the background colors are needled, create a medallion design by starting in the center and working outward, balancing color and design shapes within multiple borders. This is a versatile design and provides endless possibilities.

Cut two pieces of pre-felt, each 21 inches square. To lend durability to this pillow, you will be needling through both layers. (The pre-felt starts out larger than the pillow form to account for shrinkage during the wet felting process as well as the extra fabric needed for sewing it all together.)

Begin drawing the background geometry by creating a border around the pre-felt. Use a permanent marker and a yardstick. Place the yardstick 1 inch in from the edge and hold it in place as you trace both sides of the yardstick all the way around your piece, ensuring that your layout will be symmetrical. Creating this border gives you a framework in which to work, adds an additional opportunity for color, and provides a trimming edge.

Use a round template, such as a lampshade or a bowl, to trace a circle in the center of the box. In this sample project, I used a lampshade with a 16-inch diameter, and then a 13-inch bowl for the inner circle. Whatever you choose for a stencil, use a ruler to be sure it is centered properly within your box.

Any size stencil combination will work with the flexibility of a medallion design. The entire surface will be needled, so any mistakes you make with the marker will be covered. Use a permanent marker in order to prevent smudging and the possibility of the ink bleeding through to the surface of your design.

DESIGN TIP:

The stencil markings you outlined provide a clearly defined design area with multiple opportunities to play with color and design changes within each border. Mistakes may be corrected easily, so don't be afraid to experiment.

Choose the background colors and needle them first. Cover the entire design area, joining the colors right up to each other and needling them down tightly.

This is the groundwork for the details, which will be needled on top. Since the background colors in this example are dark, I needled the details in lighter colors, providing contrast and adding definition to the design. Use a ruler to find the center of the design area and mark it by needling some fiber in a circle about the size of a quarter.

Once the center is marked, needle evenly spaced rounded petals or triangles, and then continue working the design outward.

Stay flexible with your color choices and design shapes until you have found the right combination. There is no secret formula, just playful discovery.

There are always opportunities to change or correct things as you create felt. If you change your mind about a color, needle the new color over it rather than pulling it out if it has been needled securely.

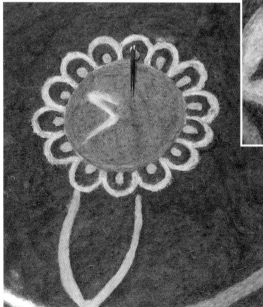

Build up layers of color and detail

Corner design

Refer to your ruler often to keep the design shapes symmetrical.

. . . .

Remember, to prevent the pre-felt from adhering to the needling board it must be rotated frequently by gently lifting it up. If the square shape becomes distorted, tug it gently back into shape before continuing.

. . . .

The designs are simple shapes that are made more elaborate by the many details added on top. By layering the details on top of the background shapes you will avoid any gaps between color changes.

To maintain a balance of color, use some of the same colors within each border as you work outward. If you get frustrated trying to choose a design, a shape, or the perfect color, work on a different area until the answer reveals itself. It is helpful to work each area a little at a time, maintaining some consistency in design shapes and continuity of color.

Once the design is needled, outline the background geometry with black. A dark outline between color changes makes the design crisp and provides greater contrast. It also covers up any gaps between the colors.

A multi-needled tool is great for doing the final touch-up. The more needles your tool has, the more challenging it is to penetrate the felt. It helps if you stand up while you needle with a tool like this, as you will have the weight of your body behind you to help push the tool through the pre-felt. Add more color if any area is too thin.

The outside border will be the trimming and sewing edge. Be sure your pre-felt has remained square before you begin wet felting.

Needling the edge

Check to see if the design has been needled enough. Run your hand over the surface to check for shifting fibers; if you see any movement, needle that area down a little more. Turn the pillow over. Felting needles push some of the fiber through to the back, so the design should be distinguishable. If you see a weak area, turn it back over and needle that spot some more. Holding it up to the light will also reveal any weak areas. The more your design has been needled, the better the end result will be.

As you work on larger projects, it becomes more difficult to wet felt with only your hand, and additional equipment is helpful.

Refer to the wet felting section at the beginning of the book to learn how to prepare a space for wet felting and how to make your own felt roller.

Lay your needled pillow face down on top of the plastic in your wet felting area. By tightening the back of the pillow first, you can minimize the amount of fibers migrating to the surface.

Fill a bowl with a few cups of hot water and keep it next to your felt. Scrunch up a plastic grocery bag in your fist and submerge it in the hot water, then place the bag over the pillow. Press down, releasing the trapped water onto the pre-felt. Repeat this process until the entire piece is saturated. The lanolin in wool is naturally resistant to water, so pressing it pushes out the air and forces in the water.

If the piece is saturated enough, water should pool around your fingers when you press down. Put soap on the palm of your hand and glide it over the surface, gently at first, then more aggressively. The movement of your hand is agitating the wool, forcing the fiber strands to entangle and tighten, creating felt. If your hand stops gliding smoothly, add more soap.

- -

Your pre-felt will shrink during the wet felting process as the fibers tighten together. To be sure it maintains its shape, use an even amount of pressure in all areas, checking periodically with a yardstick. If one area shrinks more and distorts the shape, try applying more agitation to the opposite area.

- -

You may apply more pressure as the fibers begin to tighten. Pushing out a little excess water here and there can help the felting process. If there is too much water, the strands of fibers may swim right past each other and their scales will not have a chance to become entangled. Not having enough water can also impede the process and cause a roughened surface on your felt, so be sure it is saturated through. To test, apply a little pressure to be sure the water is still pooling around your fingers. Add more hot water and soap anytime it is needed.

If you are using a felt roller, the textured surface of your plastic mat will be doing the work, which will alleviate the pressure on your hands. If you are using a different textured tool, always begin gently until you are certain your pre-felt is thoroughly saturated and enough soap has been applied for easy and smooth movement of your tool.

Whether you are using your hands, a felting roller, or another textured tool, continue wet felting until your pillow measures about 20 inches square.

There are many variables when it comes to the shrinkage rate of wool, and these are explained in the wet felting section at the beginning of the book.

Rinse the pillow thoroughly to remove the soap, press with a hot iron on both sides (using a cloth between the felt and the iron), and lay the pillow flat to dry.

If you find that the pillow is no longer square, you may try stretching it into shape while it is wet. If it needs more than a little tweak, wet it out again and continue to felt the areas that need more attention, bringing it back to a square.

Depending on the quality of your pre-felt, the base wool may migrate through to the design area. If that occurs, shave the surface with a razor, applying the same pressure you would use on your skin. Clean up the shaved fibers using a lint roller.

It is never too late to touch up the design with the needles if necessary.

Once the pillow top is dry, trim the edges square.

To finish your project, cut the piece of backing fabric to the same size as the felt. With right sides facing, stitch along three edges and turn it right side out. Insert a pillow form and stitch the bottom to close it.

Monochromatic Table Centerpiece

This is a great example of adapting embroidery and graphed needlework patterns to suit tapestry needle felting. The complexity of the design looks stunning, even when completed with just one color, and the precision of the needle allows you to get beautiful detail. Introducing animals to a felt tapestry adds life to it, especially when they are in motion. You will see how the project uses simple shapes to create elaborate effect.

Materials

Wool

Pre-felt, 15 x 28 inches or size desired. This project used a handmade pre-felt base using wool from www.goodshepherdyarn.com; the beautiful green color is called Picholine.

Carded needling fiber. I used fiber in Sand, by Harrisville Designs.

Felting Needle

38 triangular

Centered design

The pre-felt for this project measures 15 x 28 inches, but any size will work. Always start a bit larger than your desired dimensions to account for the shrinkage that will occur when you do the finish wet felting and to allow for a trimming edge. Use two layers of manufactured or one layer of handmade pre-felt for this project. Use a needling board that is approximately the size of your pre-felt.

With a yardstick, create an even border all the way around. Leave about 1 inch on the outside edge for trimming once the wet felting is complete. A metallic permanent marker works best for darker colored pre-felt. Hold the yardstick in place as you trace both sides.

Use plates or bowls as stencils to draw two circles in the middle of the felt, measuring from each side and end to be sure they are centered in all directions before tracing. For this example I used a 12-inch-diameter plate to draw a circle in the center of the pre-felt. I used a 10-inch-diameter plate to draw a second circle, centered inside the first.

The more you draw on the pre-felt base, the greater the chance for permanent marks in areas that you won't be needling, so use caution.

Once the background geometry is drawn, place the pre-felt on the needling board. Use cream or white fiber and begin with a piece of carded wool about the diameter of a pencil. This will help create a consistent border as you needle over the marker lines. Pencil roving also works well, providing an even and consistent line.

Don't needle anything tightly until you are certain of its placement. With monochromatic designs, there is a negative space (the background) that will have no needling. If you want to make a change and the design has been needled tightly, it may leave a mark as you try to remove it. To fix this you could needle some of the background fiber over it, but to prevent it, don't needle the fiber tightly until you are certain of its position.

The borders were filled with a variety of designs: a Greek key pattern runs the length, small dots were needled to decorate the circumference of the center circles, and horseshoes were used on the ends. Your own design ideas can be substituted using the same techniques and any variation on the background border designs. I encourage your own artistic freedom.

The center circle lends itself beautifully to a medallion design, but to challenge your skills this project features horses and will teach you how to line up two motifs so that they are symmetrical.

Create the first horse. Don't worry about the details; get his body shape needled and add the details later. It helps to have an illustration of a horse at hand. I chose this horse from the book *4000 Animal, Bird & Fish Motifs—A Sourcebook* by Graham Leslie McCallum.

After you have created one motif, it is easy to line up the second motif. Use a ruler to measure the completed horse. Measure from the tip of his nose straight out to the circumference of the circle and then straight down to the bottom of the circular border. With those two measurements you will know exactly where to begin the muzzle of the second horse. You can use the same measuring technique for his tail, the top of his head, or any other points on his body. The more points of reference you have, the more identically aligned your motifs will be.

Adding borders and center motifs

Fill in any empty space with a variety of motifs, either floral or geometric. Add the eye, the mane, the mouth, and any other details to the horses.

DESIGN TIP:

Guardian animals are a traditional theme in many ancient textiles, and the center vase in this design represents the Tree of Life or the Holy Grail.

These ideas transcend geography and time, as so many cultures used the same idea, varying designs and animals to suit cultural differences throughout history.

I began the side (or end) portions of the design by finding the center and needling the vase first. The vase is centered and extends straight up the middle. Notice that it begins at the bottom as a triangle, an oval shape makes up the body of the vase, and an upside-down triangle is the top. I used some elongated "S" shapes for the handles. The vase is a great way to create a center between animals or other motifs because the flowers and vines can be twisted into any shape to accommodate the design area and fill in any blank spots.

The birds also began as simple shapes. Again, don't worry about the details, but get the basic

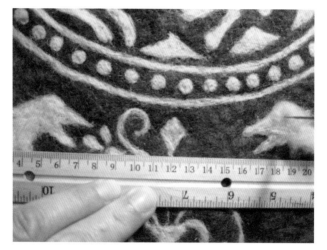

Whispy bits of wool become intricate motifs

shape down. The opposite side is a mirror image; use the center vase as the point of reference in lining them up with the ruler.

Once the birds and the vase are in position, the rest of the area can be filled with vines, leaves, and flowers. They look so elaborate, and you are an expert at making them by now!

When you begin the design on the other end, don't worry about making it exactly match the first. The beauty of a handmade tapestry design is the irregularity of it. Just begin in the center with the vase, and the rest will be beautiful no matter what shape it takes.

Check to see if it has been needled enough. Remember, the more it has been needled, the better the end result. Run your hand over the surface to check for shifting fibers; if you see any movement, needle that area down a little more.

Turn the felt over. Felting needles push the fiber through to the back, so the design should be clearly distinguishable. If you see a weak area, turn it back over and needle that spot some more.

Set up a wet felting area following the instructions in the beginning of the book.

Lay the design face down on the plastic. By laying it face down, you will tighten the back fibers first. Saturate the pre-felt with hot water. Fill a bowl with a few cups of hot water and keep it next to your design. Scrunch up a plastic grocery bag in your fist and submerge it in the hot water, then place the bag over the tapestry. Press down, releasing the trapped water onto the pre-felt. Repeat this process until the entire piece is saturated. The lanolin in wool is naturally resistant to water so pressing it pushes out the air and forces in the water.

Water should pool around your fingers when you press down. Put soap on the palm of your hand and glide it over the surface, gently at first, then more aggressively. The continuous movement of your hand is agitating the wool, forcing the fiber strands to entangle and tighten, and creating felt. If your hand stops gliding smoothly, add more soap.

Your pre-felt will shrink during the wet felt process as the fibers tighten together. To be sure it maintains its shape use an even amount of pressure in all areas, checking periodically with a ruler. If one area shrinks more and distorts the pre-felt, try applying more agitation to the opposite areas to bring it back into shape.

You may apply more pressure as the fibers begin to tighten. Pushing out a little excess water here and there can help the felting process. Add more hot water or soap anytime it is needed.

If you are using a felt roller, the textured surface of the wrap will be doing the work, which will alleviate the pressure on your hands. If you are using a different textured tool, always begin gently until you are certain your pre-felt is thoroughly saturated and enough soap has been applied for easy and smooth movement.

Continue wet felting until your table centerpiece measures about 14 x 27 inches. The tapestry should shrink down approximately 1 inch horizontally and 1 inch vertically.

Rinse the felt, removing the soap thoroughly, and use a hot iron on both sides of the centerpiece to flatten and smooth the fibers. Place a cloth between the iron and the felt to prevent burning and to absorb some of the moisture. Lay it flat to dry. Trimming with scissors provides a nice clean edge, but if you prefer, the natural edges are quite beautiful also. After trimming, the finished dimensions should be about 13 x 26 inches.

When your centerpiece needs to be cleaned, wash it by hand in warm soapy water.

Tree of Life Tapestry

*T*his is a lively tapestry project that will show you how to create harmony by balancing color and design. You will experiment with some shading techniques and some new design shapes. A book of flower illustrations is useful for design ideas.

Materials

Wool

Pre-felt in a dark color
Carded fiber in colors of your choice

Felting Needle

38 triangular

Finishing

2 inch x 18 inch fabric strip to sew on the
   back
20-inch-long dowel rod

For this tapestry to drape nicely on the wall, begin with two layers of pre-felt measuring 17 x 23 inches. Darker colored pre-felt will really make your design stand out.

Create a border around the tapestry first. This will help you to square your piece and will give you a clear visual of the design area before you begin needling. Use a permanent marker and a yardstick. Place the yardstick about ¼ inch in from the edge and hold it in place as you trace both sides all the way around, ensuring that the layout process is symmetrical. The border will frame the tapestry and provide a little extra room for trimming. It will also be another opportunity to add a color.

A needling board the size of the pre-felt is helpful, especially as you tackle larger projects. The insulation board provides firm resistance and will allow you to rest your elbow and wrist on the surface as you work. Remember to periodically lift your project gently off the needling board.

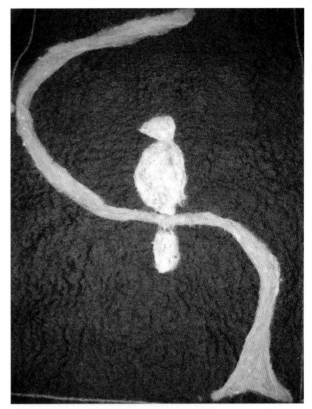

The Tree of Life design begins as a simple design shape starting in the bottom right corner. Taper the trunk of the tree and begin the first bend at about 5 or 6 inches up. The tree branch meanders to the other side of the pre-felt before bending upward again.

This gives the bird a perch near the center of the tapestry, which is where the focal point should be. The bird begins with simple shapes— an oval for his body, a circle for his head, and a rectangle for his tail feathers. Needle the fiber in the approximate position, but don't needle it tightly yet. You may need to make adjustments as you progress.

Begin the flower clusters by creating vines that extend down toward the bottom and up to the

Adding vines and flowers

middle. Follow along with this design until you get comfortable filling up the space with your own designs.

I used several shades of green and yellow to create the tree and its vines. Using dabs of color within the design shapes can create shading and enhance the design by making the foliage more realistic.

On the finished tapestry, notice that the same colors appear in different clusters. This was planned so that the reds were interspersed, so that the blues were not too close to each other, so that the whites were spread out, and so on. The balance is harmonious. As you begin creating your clusters of flowers, think about your color choices and how to balance them as you go.

There are many opportunities in this project to experiment with flower shapes and shading. Try poking a dab of a lighter or darker shade close to the center of the flower to create a more realistic effect.

Another way to create shading is by spreading a few wispy strands of color over another color.

Use vines to extend the clusters of simple flower shapes out to the corners of the design. Fill in blank spaces with leaves and curlicue vines.

The tree branch extends to the far left of the pre-felt and begins bending upward. There is not enough space to put in a cluster here, so you could use a fern design that will fill the space perfectly and lead your design upward to the next group of flowers.

Bird details

Add detail to the bird by needling a wing in a different color than the body. Layer some color over his breast by wisping a few strands of fiber over the base color.

Create an eye for the bird by using a few strands of black fiber and needling in the same spot repeatedly.

Continue filling in the blank areas with bunches of flowers and vines, using leaves and small shoots of curling vines to fill up the blank spots.

The only thing left to needle is the border. Choose a color that you used in the tapestry to frame the scene. Use a multi-needled tool, if you have one, to complete this last bit of needling.

Check to make sure you have needled enough by turning the piece over. If the design is clearly distinguishable on the back, it is ready for wet felting.

As you work on larger projects it becomes more difficult to wet felt with your hand, and additional equipment is helpful.

Refer to the wet felting section in the beginning of the book to learn how to prepare a space for wet felting and for ideas and tools for making the wet felting process faster and easier. A felt roller is the most useful tool for many of the projects in this book.

Place the tapestry face down on top of the plastic. By tightening the back first, you can minimize the amount of fiber that migrates to the surface.

Fill a bowl with a few cups of hot water and keep it next to your felt. Scrunch up a plastic grocery bag in your fist and submerge it in the hot water, then place the bag over the tapestry. Press down, releasing the trapped water onto the pre-felt. Repeat this process until the entire piece is saturated. The lanolin in wool is naturally resistant to water so pressing it pushes out the air, and a little soap will help break through the surface and assist the saturation process.

When the project is saturated enough, water should pool around your fingers when you press down. Put soap on the palm of your hand and glide it over the surface, gently at first, then more aggressively. The continuous motion of your hand is agitating the fibers, causing them to interlock and create felt. If your hand stops gliding smoothly, add more soap.

....

Your pre-felt will shrink during the wet felting process as the fibers tighten together. To be sure it maintains its shape, use an even amount of pressure in all areas, checking periodically with a yardstick. If one area shrinks more and distorts the shape, try applying more agitation to the opposite area.

....

You may apply more pressure as the fibers begin to tighten. Pushing out a little excess water here and there can help the felting process. If there is too much water, the strands of fibers may swim right past each other and their scales will not have a chance to become entangled. Not having enough water can also impede the process and cause a roughened surface on your felt, so be sure it is saturated through, applying a little pressure to be sure the water is pooling around your fingers. Add more hot water and soap anytime it is needed.

If you are using a felt roller, the textured surface of your wrap will be doing the work, which will alleviate the pressure on your hands. If you are using a different textured tool, always begin gently

until you are certain your pre-felt is thoroughly saturated and enough soap has been applied for easy and smooth movement of your tool.

Whether you are using your hands, a felting roller, or another textured tool, continue wet felting until your tapestry measures about 16 x 22 inches. Keep a yardstick handy to measure your project as it shrinks and to be sure it stays squared.

Rinse the tapestry thoroughly to remove the soap, and then press with a hot iron on both sides, placing a cloth between the felt and the iron to prevent burning and to absorb some of the water. Lay it flat to dry. Trim all the edges square.

HELPFUL HINT:

If you find the tapestry is distorted, try stretching it into shape while it is wet. If it needs more than a little tweak, wet it all out again and felt the areas that need more attention, bringing it back into shape.

It is never too late to touch up the design with the needles if necessary.

To hang your tapestry, sew a strip of fabric to the back of the felt, creating a channel that you can slide a dowel through. Tie a piece of ribbon on either end of the dowel, hang in a prominent place, and admire your beautiful handiwork!

Landscape Tapestry

*I*f you have already completed some of the projects illustrated in this book, then you are skilled at using the needles and you are able to create balance with both color and design. This project will challenge you to compose an action scene—a landscape— with a story to tell. This tapestry, The Peaceable Kingdom, *has a lot of interesting activity going on and is ambitious both in size and complexity. It uses animals and people to create a tale in which every character is in motion.*

Materials

Wool

White pre-felt
Carded wool in colors of your choice. I
   used Harrisville Designs colors Black
   Cherry, Oatmeal, Sand, Russet, Scarlet,
   Topaz, Woodsmoke, Loden, Teak, Wal-
   nut, Hemlock, Cypress, Straw, Lilac,
   Black, Lime, Tundra, Garnet, and Grass.

Felting Needle

38 triangular
Multi-needle tools

Finishing

Dowel rod
Strip of fabric 3 inches wide and 35 inches
   long
Binding cloth

Multi-needled tools and a needling board that is at least the width of the pre-felt are vital with the increased size of this project. They will both help to alleviate potential strain to your hand.

This scene began with a piece of handmade pre-felt that measured 34 x 40 inches. If you are using machine-made pre-felt, you should use at least two layers to be sure it will hang nicely on the wall.

As you have learned from the previous projects, the design process involves creating a background first. With a yardstick and a permanent marker, draw a 2-inch border around the outside. Adding a border around the outside edge allows you to begin with a squared framework, adds an additional opportunity for color, provides a trimming edge, and frames the design.

Use a permanent marker to lay out the landscape if you like. The entire surface will be needled, so any mistakes you make with the

When you begin a landscape tapestry, it is helpful to have an idea of where you are headed. Sketching out ideas on paper is useful, even if it is simple stick figures. It will give you a fundamental idea of where everything will be placed, and you can save your artistic talents for the needling rather than the drawing. Changes do occur, however, and it is important to be flexible as your masterpiece progresses and the story unfolds.

marker will be covered. Follow along with this design or create any variation on it that you find pleasing. Needle the background colors first; the details will be needled over the background later. Use your multi-needled tool for covering large areas. The more needles your tool has, the more challenging it is to penetrate the felt. Standing up while you needle is helpful, as you will have the weight of your body behind you to help push the tool through the pre-felt.

Once the backdrop is needled down, the action begins. Remember to stay flexible as you work; your ideas will evolve and change as you progress. The process requires contemplation and patience.

This tapestry was worked from top to bottom, but you may start wherever you like.

The castle, the stones, and the cliffs were all created with a light beige color as the base. I added a few wispy strands of black, brown, grey, flesh, and purple over the beige to break up the monotony of a single color, adding texture and dimension to the overall effect. A few strands of brown fiber help to delineate the castle bricks. The flags on top of the castle added a pleasing splash of color in that corner, creating a more balanced landscape and leading the eye upward. The fountain and the moat were not planned, but adding them produced a harmonious balance by bringing the color of the ocean water from the left over to the right side of the tapestry.

The upper left corner of the tapestry looked dull, so I created another dragon in the water to pester a passing ship. Add some waves to the ocean with a slightly darker shade of blue and make the dragon appear as if he is weaving through the water. With all of the main subjects complete, fill in the blank spots with any number of details including rocks, flowers, fences, grazing animals, trees, people, and even shrubbery. Add some roads wherever you would like throughout the scene.

I recommend outlining each motif to provide crisp, clean edges and make each design shape more prominent. It also fills in any gap where two colors meet. Once the wool has been needled tightly, use black fiber to define the shapes. Whatever colors you decide to use, they will look amazing when you outline them and will make your design come to life. Remember that if you are unsatisfied with any part of your design, simply needle some background fiber over it and start again!

People, animals, and foliage are life. The more of these that you have in your tapestry, the more life your finished design will have. For this scene, the gentleman on horseback encountering the young ladies on the path is the main

theme, the foreground, and will be located in approximately the bottom center of the tapestry. This central design is framed by a tree on either side. A tree canopy lends a fairy tale quality to any landscape because it gives the impression that the viewer is peeking into the scene from a hidden location. It also adjusts the perspective and adds dimension by demonstrating how close the viewer is to the scene at hand, compared to how far away the distant trees are. Make your characters active—gathering flowers, harvesting fruit, hunting, or visiting with one another. In the foreground there is yet more space to fill, and that is where I placed rocks, flowers, a few bushels of apples, a pile of gathered logs, and some fallen fruit on the ground— all details that lend realism to the scene.

Stand back and take a look at your tapestry to see what details are lacking. I added a school of fish, some waves, and teeth for the dragons; a herd of deer having a snack in the kingdom garden; a lady on the cliff top tossing apples to the dragon below and another lady walking along the

road in the background; shrubbery to fill in an empty spot here and there—all came together to create dimension and add interest to the panorama.

DESIGN TIP:

The perspective is awkward and the design shapes are rudimentary, but the scene reveals the beauty of everyday life. That is the nature of folk art. Use your imagination; draw upon stories you have read, places you have been, or the natural world around you to create unique and beautiful art.

When you are satisfied with your scene, check to see if your tapestry has been needled enough. Run your hand over the surface to check for shifting fibers; if you see any movement, needle that area down a little more. Turn the tapestry over. Felting needles push some of the fiber through to the back, and the design should be distinguishable on the back. If you see a weak area, turn it back over and needle that spot some more. Remember, the more your design has been needled, the better the end result.

Wet felting a piece this large can present some challenges. If your wet felting area is not big enough, consider setting up a table outside; or if you are using a felt roller, once it is saturated and rolled up, you can put it in the bathtub and roll it with your feet.

A roller assembly is a great help in maintaining squared edges, getting the wet felting done faster, and allowing you to better manage a piece this size. Instructions on how to make your own roller assembly are located in the wet felting section at the beginning of the book.

Set up your wet felting work station according to the instructions. Lay the tapestry face down on the plastic. Fill a bowl with a few cups of hot tap water and keep it close to your felt. Scrunch up a plastic grocery bag in your fist and dip it in the water. Press the wet bag down onto the tapestry, pushing the water into the needled design. Repeat this process until the piece is saturated.

Be sure that water pools around your fingers when you press down. Put soap on the palm of your hand and glide it over the surface in a circular or back and forth motion, gently at first then more aggressively. Your hand is agitating the fibers and forcing them to entangle with one another, creating felt. If your hand stops gliding smoothly, add more soap.

No matter what tools you are using to help you make felt, it is always best to begin the wet felting with your hands to be sure the entire piece is well saturated. Your pre-felt will shrink during the wet felt process as the fibers tighten together. To be sure it maintains its shape, keep it flat and use an equal amount of pressure in all areas, checking periodically with a yardstick. If one area shrinks more and distorts the shape, try applying agitation to the opposite area to bring it back in line.

Continue wet felting until the tapestry has tightened and shrunk down a minimum of 1 inch.

HELPFUL HINT:

If your tapestry has become distorted after the wet felting is complete, try reshaping it by tugging gently while it is wet. This may work for small tweaks and alignments, but because of the elasticity in wool, if it has become too distorted, you should saturate it again with hot soapy water and felt it some more.

Rinse the tapestry thoroughly to remove the soap. Use a hot iron and press both sides of the felt tapestry to flatten and smooth the fibers. Place a cloth between the iron and the felt to prevent burning and to absorb some of the moisture. It is never too late to touch it up with the needles if needed. Lay the tapestry flat to dry.

Once it is dry, trim the piece, using your sharp scissors and yardstick to maintain straight edges and crisp lines. Touch up any loose fibers with the needles if you need to. You can shave the surface with a disposable razor; clean up any fuzzy pieces with a lint roller.

To clean your tapestry, wash it by hand in warm soapy water.

I bound the edges with double-fold bias tape quilt binding (pre-folded) using a sewing machine to apply it around the outer edge. Sew the fabric strip along the top back of the tapestry, creating a channel that you can slide the dowel through. Tie a ribbon, making a knot on each end of the dowel. Hang your tapestry on the wall and admire your lovely needlework!

Persian Rug

*T*his project will challenge you with its seemingly complex design and with the size and thickness of the pre-felt base you will be needling. Because you will be felting for durability, it will require more upper body strength.

Materials

Wool

A single layer of handmade pre-felt or a
double layer of machine-made pre-felt in
any color
Carded wool in colors of your choice. I
used Harrisville Designs fiber in Midnight
Blue, Russet, Poppy, and Jade for the
background, and Tundra, Mustard, Teak,
Bluegrass, Woodsmoke, Hemlock, and
Topaz for the details.
Pencil roving in Orange and Turquoise

Felting needles

36 or 38 triangular
Multi-needle tools

Finishing

Binding fabric for outer edges

DESIGN TIP:

This is another project inspired by a Persian rug. The
multiple borders take up a good portion of the space
and allow for many opportunities to play with color
and design.

The complex motifs of the original rug were
reduced to simple shapes that translated easily and
beautifully into needle felt.

*T*he design process begins by creating the background geometry. All of your design tools will
come into play, and a few other essential items—
multi-needled tools, a large needling board, and a
felt roller—will help you create your rug.

This rug began with a piece of handmade pre-
felt wool measuring 31 x 37 inches and weighing
1 pound. Use as many layers of pre-felt as you
need to approximate that weight.

Look beyond all the daunting detail of the original woven rugs and focus on the background.
You cannot help but notice the many borders that
frame these elaborate rugs, all leading to the center. Each border offers you an opportunity for
color and design change which will make your
finished rug more elaborate.

Use a permanent marker and a yardstick to lay
out the background geometry. Lay the yardstick
on the pre-felt about ¼ inch in from the outside
edge. This will leave a small edge for trimming
and binding at the end. With the yardstick on top
of the pre-felt, trace both sides of it. This is the

first border (Midnight Blue). Draw another box of the same width inside the first to create the second border (Russet). Move the yardstick inside that box and draw the third border (Jade). All three borders are the same width and are made by tracing both sides of the yardstick. Depending on the size of your felt, you could have the opportunity for more borders of varying width leading to your central design.

Find the center of the felt by measuring in from the last box you drew. Draw, and then needle, a diamond shape measuring about 3 inches on each side (Jade) at that spot. Needle a wide border around that, so that now the diamond is 8 inches long on each side (Midnight Blue). Next, create a 1-inch border around that (Jade), as illustrated.

Use a ruler to draw the stepped design within the three borders. Keep your lines straight but do not worry about the exact dimensions. I used a 7-inch-long line centered on each end and a 10-inch-long line centered on each side to begin. In this example, each stair in the red area is about 2 inches wide, creating three steps in each corner, but any size will work. Yours will be beautiful regardless of what widths you use.

Russet is a beautiful shade of brick red, but it looked too dark. I used some Poppy red and wisped a few strands over the Russet, creating a subtle color change with a mottled appearance that helped to brighten it up.

Fill in the rest of the background geometry by needling the chosen colors down tightly. Lay them out evenly but thickly and use a multi-needled tool to secure the fiber well. I used about 6 ounces of wool for the foundation colors in this rug. The details will be needled on top of the background colors. Remember to lift your pre-felt gently off the needling board to rotate it as you progress.

In the smaller projects, you were advised to use caution in the amount of fiber you applied. This was to minimize stress on your hand and to demonstrate what a few strands of fiber can accomplish. For this project you will be layering the colors thickly to build up the foundation. A rug will need more durability than the previous projects, and the weak areas will show wear first.

Some of the multi-needled tools can be cumbersome to handle and may require a great deal of force to get them through such thick pre-felt. The process will be much easier if you are able to

Persian rug details

stand up so that you have your body weight behind the tool as you penetrate the pre-felt.

Needle the background colors down tightly. Outline each change of color. Pencil roving may be used for this task, as it provides a consistent line and is easy to work with.

Now for the details—follow along with this example or create your own design!

Create detail within each background color. Simple shapes and color changes can look dynamic. Petals, vines, and medallions are easy shapes to create and look intricate. Use a sunrise or starburst design to brighten up the corners.

I played around with some ideas and experimented with the details until a pattern of color and design emerged that I found pleasing. I had a picture of a Shiraz rug that I was trying to emulate, extracting the intricate woven designs and modifying them to suit this needle felting project.

The design motifs may be translated into simple shapes like triangles, diamonds, circles, chevrons, and squares. Try pointing them in different directions to create the impression of complexity. Placing one shape inside another can look elaborate. A circle in a square outlined in pencil roving filled small spaces in the background. The hook design that emanates from the diamond shapes is an easy way to fill in some space.

I moved back and forth from the borders to the center to break up the monotony. I stood back occasionally to view the progress to be certain I was creating a piece pleasing in both color and design. Create continuity in your rug by balancing your color scheme. Use some of the same colors in different ways for each border you created.

The four Midnight Blue corners contain a tree design which is simple to create. Begin with a small triangle at the bottom and needle a line going to the top. I covered the top with a circle of wool, and then I needled the branches extending out the sides of the center line. I still had more design space to fill, so I added a couple of smaller trees and a few random floating dots.

As always, be sure to check that your work is needled enough by running your hand over it to check for shifting fibers and turning it over to make sure the design is visible on the back. Weak areas in needling will result in weak areas of wear, but you can always touch it up with the needles at any time during its life.

Set up your wet felting work station according to the instructions in the beginning of the book. Lay the rug face down on the plastic. By laying it face down, you will tighten the back fibers first and minimize the amount of fiber migrating to the front.

You will need to saturate the rug with hot water. Fill a bowl with a few cups of hot tap water and keep it next to your felt. Scrunch the plastic grocery bag in your fist and dip it in the water. Press the wet bag down onto the rug, pushing the water into the pre-felt. Repeat this process until is the pre-felt is saturated.

To check that the piece is saturated enough, be sure water pools around your fingers when you press down. Put soap on the palm of your hand and glide it over the surface in a circular or back and forth motion, gently at first, then more aggressively. The continuous motion of your hand is agitating the fibers and forcing them to entangle with one another, eventually creating felt. If your hand stops gliding smoothly, add more soap. No matter what tools you are using to help you make felt, it is always best to begin with your hand to be sure the entire piece is well saturated.

Your pre-felt will shrink during the wet felt process as the fibers tighten together. To be sure that it maintains square edges, use an even amount of pressure in all areas, checking periodically with a yardstick. If one area shrinks more and distorts the shape, try applying more agitation to the opposite areas to bring it back in line.

Use your roller assembly to help with the agitation of this project. Roll it, and then roll it some more. Unroll it and reroll it from the other end. Do this for a very long time. With the other projects in the book that you wet felted, you were not striving for the durability of hardened felt, but this time you are; it will take longer and require more strength. Always add more soap and hot water as needed. Continue until it has tightened and shrunk a minimum of 1 inch.

Rinse the rug thoroughly to remove the soap. One way to do this is to put it in the washing machine on a rinse cycle, but **don't let it agi-**

tate**, simply rinse and spin. The bathtub is also a great place to rinse by hand, and you can leave it there to let the water drain off.

If your rug has become distorted after the wet felting is complete, try reshaping it by tugging gently while it is wet. This may work for small tweaks and alignments, but because of the elasticity in wool, if it has become badly distorted, you should saturate it again with hot soapy water and felt it some more.

While it is still wet, use a hot iron to press both sides of the rug to flatten and smooth the fibers. Place a cloth between the iron and the felt to prevent burning and to absorb some of the moisture. It is never too late to touch it up with the needles if needed. Lay the rug flat to dry.

Trim the edges, using your yardstick to keep the alignment squared and sharp scissors for a crisp line. After the needling and wet felting were complete and the piece was dry, the example had a final measurement of 30 x 36 inches and weighed 1 pound 9 ounces.

DESIGN TIP:

The background geometry and design motifs were inspired by an antique rug from Shiraz, Iran, and I added a few Turkish embellishments that I liked. When I showed it to my friend, she immediately said, "Oh what a lovely southwestern design; it looks very Native American."

The fascinating thing about design motifs is how they transformed as they traveled around the world and came in contact with different cultures. The designs were adapted to fit different mediums—not just textiles, but pottery, painting, and many other forms of decorative art.

Sew on a border to lend durability to the edges. On this piece, I used double-fold bias tape quilt binding and a sewing machine to attach it around the outer edge.

If your rug needs to be cleaned, it is easily washed by hand in warm soapy water. With gentle use your rug will last for many years. Best of all, if it shows wear, it can always be touched up with the needles and felted again.

Gathering Fruit. *The simple action of gathering fruit sets the scene, and the story comes to life with the sweet serenade by friendly birds.*

Templates

Enlarge templates to your preferred size. Remember to account for shrinkage that occurs during wet felting.

Sugar Skull

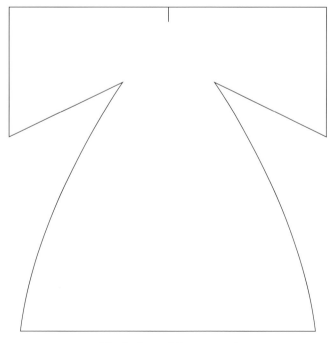

Choir Angel Ornament

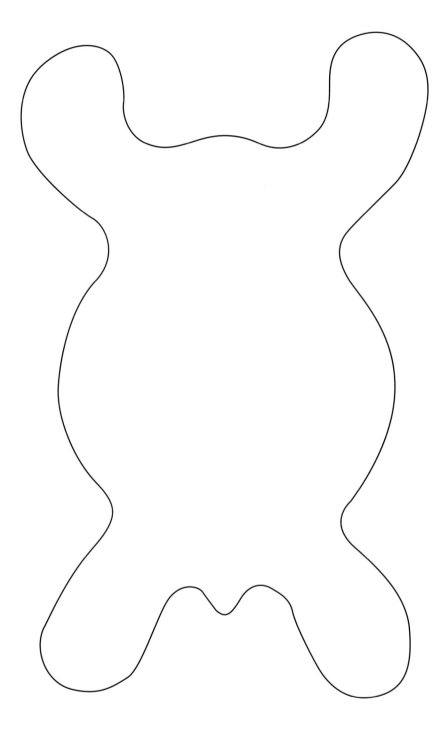

Bear Mug Rug

Dragon Table Centerpiece

Maple Leaf Coaster

Felting Supply Sources

Specialty Suppliers

The Spinning Studio
1062 South Road
Bradford, Vermont 05033
802-222-9240
neysa.russo@live.com
Felting rollers, fiber, silks, pre-felt, felting kits
www.thespinning studio.com

Harrisville Designs
4 Mill Alley
Harrisville, New Hampshire 03450
www.harrisvilledesigns.com
Carded wool in a broad range of colors

Mielkes Fiber Arts
N4826 21st Ave
Mauston, WI 53948
www.mielkesfiberarts.com
Assortment of great felting supplies

Northeast Fiber Arts Center
7531 Williston Road
Williston, Vermont 05495
www.northeastfiberarts.com
Complete line of wet felting and needle felting
supplies

New England Felting Supply
84 Cottage Street
Easthampton, Massachusetts
www.feltingsupply.com
Complete line of wet felting and needle felting
supplies

Port Fiber
50 Cove St.
Portland, ME 04101
www.portfiber.com
Beautiful colors of pre-felt

Zeilingers Wool
1130 Weiss St.
Frankenmuth, MI 48734
www.zwool.com
Custom batt processing, pencil roving, wool batts

Other supplies

AC Moore
Basic felting supplies and general craft materials

Jo-Ann Fabric and Craft
Pillow forms, snaps, dowels, backing fabric, binding tape, needles, general craft supplies

Michaels
Basic felting supplies and general craft materials

Susan's Fiber Shop
N250 County Rd. A
Columbus, WI 53925
www.susansfiber.com
Interesting assortment of great tools, loads of
books

Bibliography

Wet Felting Technique

Spark, Patricia. *Fundamentals of Feltmaking*. Washington: Shuttle Craft Books, 1989.

Claessen, Marlie. *Felting*. Lochem, Holland: Louet b.v., 1981.

Textile Inspiration

Johnstone, Pauline. *Greek Island Embroidery*. London: Alec Tiranti Ltd., 1961.

Volbach, W. Fritz. *Early Decorative Textiles*. Middlesex, England: Hamlyn Publishing Group, 1969.

Fassett, Kaffe. *Glorious Inspiration for Needlepoint & Knitting*. New York: Sterling Publishing, 1991

Liebetrau, Preben. *Oriental Rugs in Color*. New York: Macmillan Publishing Co., Inc., 1963.

Bath, Virginia C. *Embroidery Masterworks*. Chicago: Henry Regnery Company, 1972.

Design & Motif Inspiration

McCallum, Graham L. *4000 Animal, Bird & Fish Motifs*. London: Batsford, 2005.

Bossert, Helmuth T. *Treasury of Historic Folk Ornament*. Mineola, New York: Dover Publications, Inc., 1996.

Grafton, Carol B., ed. *400 Floral Motifs for Designers, Needleworkers and Craftspeople*. Mineola, New York: Dover Publications, Inc., 1986.

Harrell, Betsy. *Anatolian Knitting Designs*. Istanbul, Turkey: Redhouse Press, 1981.

Eiland III, Murray. *Starting to Collect Antique Oriental Rugs*. Suffolk, England: Antique Collectors Club Ltd., 2003.